How to Collect
French Fashion Dolls

Mildred and Vernon Seeley

About the Authors

Mildred and Vernon Seeley have been involved in doll making and doll collecting for nearly 40 years. They were the former owners of Seeley's Ceramics in Oneonta, New York. Both are noted authorities on doll making, antique doll appraising and doll photography. Together, they also work as consultants to doll businesses, give lectures and hold seminars all over the United States on antique dolls.

Mildred studied art, sculpture and painting and holds a master's degree in art education. She was the founder of the Doll Artisan Guild. She has also written numerous books on dolls and doll making. Mildred and Colleen (her daughter) wrote two detailed, comprehensive books on antique dolls—**Doll Collecting for Fun & Profit** and **Doll Costuming**, both published by HPBooks.

Vernon is a master mold maker and has made hundreds of molds from antique dolls, including his mold of the rare Marque doll, which was the most expensive limited-edition reproduction doll ever made. He holds degrees in science and industrial arts. He has written a textbook on ceramics and co-authored several doll books with Mildred, including **How to Collect French Bébé Dolls**, also published by HPBooks.

Photo on previous page: 13-inch doll marked *E Déposé IB,* for Barrois. Head is swivel type with flat, cobalt-blue glass eyes. Ears are pierced into head. Body is gusseted, hand-sewn leather with toes indicated by stitching. Arms and hands are leather with wired fingers. Old human-hair wig is hand-tied. Simple cocoa-wool dress could be mothermade or replacement. Top is fitted, and skirt is full, in style of 1860s. Dress is trimmed with brown velvet. Doll wears mitts on her hands. She has hat (not shown) of dark-brown velvet with black feather. Underwear is linen with fine eyelet trim. Hand-woven stockings are shaped. Shoes are hand-sewn, flat, slipper-type with silver buckle. Doll is also shown on page 94.

Photo on cover: Beautiful Smiler doll is dressed in lavender. She is also shown on pages 22 and 116.

Contents

Publisher: Rick Bailey; Editorial Director: Randy Summerlin; Editor: Judith Schuler; Art Director: Don Burton; Book Design & Assembly: Kathleen Koopman; Typography: Cindy Coatsworth, Michelle Carter; Book Manufacture: Anthony B. Narducci; Cover Photography: Ray Manley Studios, Tucson, Arizona; Photography: Ray Manley Studios and Mildred Seeley

HPBooks, Inc.
P.O. Box 5367, Tucson, AZ 85703   (602) 888-2150
ISBN: 0-89586-425-8
Library of Congress Catalog Card Number: 85-80114
©1985 HPBooks, Inc.   Printed in U.S.A.
1st Printing

Beginning the Search for French Fashion Dolls

A doll collector who hasn't discovered the fabulous French fashion dolls has missed one of the most challenging areas of collecting. Collecting "Parisiennes" is like transporting yourself into the past and reliving life as it was 120 years ago.

The shapely ladylike fashion dolls, with their glamorous Parisian costumes, can be compared to the lovely ladies of the period. Even their miniature accessories and doll trunks take us back in time.

The fantastic handcrafted bodies remind us there was a time when perfection of the craft, rather than time spent, was most important. And the charming bisque faces are as perfect today as the day they came from the kiln.

This book attempts to expand your horizons as a doll collector or doll admirer by calling your attention to these bisque-headed ladylike dolls, called *French fashions,* which were produced from the 1850s to the 20th century. These are the dolls that time has swallowed and collectors have forgotten.

We use the term "French fashion dolls" for dolls with shapely, lady-type figures, whether or not they are dressed in Parisian fashions. We use this term because it has been used for so long that it immediately brings to mind a certain type of doll made in France for over 50 years. We also use the term *Parisienne* for these dolls.

There are no books that deal exclusively with these antique dolls. There is no organized study collectors can use to gather information. This book is intended as a reference tool and as an inspiration to collectors who own, or wish to own, French fashion dolls. It is also written for those who study dolls but do not collect them. Photos are for collectors *and* doll artists, who want beautiful, sharp photos from which to paint. Creative costumers can copy the incredible costumes with our permission.

Our Criteria for Collecting—We collected the

Left: 15-inch Smiler is marked *2.* Ears are pierced through ear lobe. Body is wood, completely articulated at waist, hips, wrists and ankles. Couturier gown is soft, dull-green silk. It has worn through in many places, and lining is all that remains. Costume is lavishly trimmed with lace, gathering and seed pearls. Full train and bustle are edged in several laces. Gown is almost beyond saving. Doll is also shown on page 93.

French fashion dolls in this book for four reasons:

- Beauty of face and costume.
- Construction of bodies.
- Investment qualities.
- Historic value.

These may be the best guidelines for beginning collectors, as well as connoisseurs of French fashion dolls.

Fashion dolls are selected and judged by an entirely new set of rules. Many established criteria for collecting other dolls do not apply to these antiques.

Collecting adult-figured dolls in elaborate costumes appeals to a different group of collectors. Often collectors of French fashion dolls are students of history or historic costuming. The dolls also appeal to artistic collectors. Sometimes it's the joy of putting a doll in a homelike setting or using it as part of a room decor that makes it appealing.

Men often find the perfection of craftsmanship of the different bodies intriguing. And designers of fashion find them irresistible.

These dolls may be neglected today, except by knowledgeable collectors who have taken time to study what is under a costume. Fashion dolls are still available and reasonably priced. They are antiques, and we feel certain they are a good investment. Soon prices may soar, as they have with other dolls. This seems to happen when we begin to study a particular type of doll and call attention to values.

Other Reasons for Collecting—With study, you will find French fashion dolls among the most beautiful ever made. You will discover the intriguing variations in the bodies; collecting French fashions may become a passion.

The number of variations in body form and the elaborate costumes make these dolls a joy to collect. The dolls and the historic value of their trunks, with treasures and trousseaus, hold collectors spellbound.

One of the purposes of this book is to make you comfortable and knowledgeable enough to purchase one or many French fashion dolls. You will know which type of body, head and cos-

Large 28-inch E.J. Jumeau with rare, unmarked 17-inch child fashion doll. Note length of skirt and blue boots on child doll. Bustled dress is blue striped silk with silk lace.

tume you desire for your collection. You will understand markings or lack of them. You will realize the price a doll will bring and know what items dictate price. You will know where to look for dolls.

If minor repairs are needed, this book provides instructions for repair, beginning on page 125, and supplies you with names and addresses for materials, page 137. We want to convince you to invest time before dollars to increase your understanding and enjoyment in collecting French fashion dolls.

In this book, we use the term *she* when refer-

Right: Jumeau doll is pressed bisque with applied, pierced-through-lobe ears. Blue paperweight eyes have radiating lines. Mouth and cheek color are soft and light. Eyebrows are fine, and eyelashes are black. Antique hat is woven straw, lined in pale-green silk. Ribbon decoration was same color. Doll is also shown on page 24.

UFDC prize-winning black French fashion doll. Appropriate costume is original. She has distinct features and protruding upper and lower teeth. Gladyse Hillsdorf doll.

Doll wears lavender-striped silk top. Black full-skirt is trimmed with lavender to match top trim. She has all-wood body, and her head is marked *H.* Lenore Thomas doll.

ring to a collector. This is a matter of convenience, even though we realize nearly 50% of French fashion doll collectors are men. It appears many of the very best collections are owned by men.

Photos of French Fashion Dolls—We have included photos of some dolls from other collections. It was a privilege to be allowed to study and photograph Lenore Thomas' French fashion dolls. We greatly appreciate her help. Her collection contains groupings and arrangements with props and furniture that are finer than any doll museum we have visited.

Rare dolls from Gladyse Hillsdorf's collection are also included. Gladyse, who was recovering from a broken hip when we visited her, put forth a great deal of effort to help us. She is known for her knowledge of dolls and her unique, immense collection.

Photos were also sent to us from Marcia Cohen, who is associated with Cohen Auctions. Cohen Auctions always seems to have some of the finest French fashion dolls available. Many doll dealers, listed on pages 137 and 138, also helped us find certain dolls and allowed us to take pictures of their collections.

Most dolls shown in this book are from our collection. But we have included photos of dolls owned by other collectors, and in these instances, we include the name of the owner in the photo caption.

Our research has revealed many things to us, and we will prove French fashion dolls were used as toys *and* couriers of fashion. In this

Left: 26-inch swivel-headed doll, marked *F.G.*, has warped gusseted body. Original wig is blond mohair. Costume was recently made of old material and was changed from time when doll was made (1870) to 1890s' costume. Blouse is dotted Swiss, and skirt is heavy linen. Adult doll takes R.D. and Mascotte child dolls butterfly hunting in flower-covered Alps. F.G. doll is also shown on page 18.

spirit, we have photographed dolls against ships, fields and roadways from England, France, Italy, Germany and the United States. We hope the photographs will increase your joy in collecting these delightful bits of fine art.

ORIGIN OF FRENCH FASHION DOLLS

Fashion dolls—the French fashion mannequins that actually were "grands couriers de la mode" (carriers of fashion)—were made and used centuries *before* small bisque-headed lady dolls. The bisque-headed lady dolls we now call *French fashion dolls* were produced shortly *after* the introduction of porcelain in Europe. Before that time, lady fashion dolls (mannequins) were made of wood, wax, papier-mâché, cloth or a combination of these materials.

From Research by Von Boehn—From the research of Max von Boehn (translated by Josephine Nicoll) in the book *Dolls* (published in 1929), we learned early fashion dolls were *life-sized mannequins*. Their use was first recorded in 1396. Dolls were used to display the fashions of Paris and the elaborate coiffures of the day. This was before woodcuts and copper etchings were used to produce fashion plates or pictures.

These mannequins were shipped from Paris to various courts of Europe. Von Boehn found a letter from the Abbé Prevost, written in 1704, that states, "By an act of gallantry which is worthy of being noted in the chronicles of history for the benefit of the ladies, the ministers of both Courts granted a special pass to the mannequin (dolls); that pass was always respected during the times of greatest enmity experienced. On both sides, the mannequin was the one object which remained unmolested."

In other papers and letters Von Boehn also found quotes that have been important in establishing the fact these dolls were life-sized mannequins wearing full-sized clothing. Marie deMédici, second wife of King Henry IV, was eager to learn all about French fashions. From a letter the king wrote to her from Paris, we learned "that you wish to have samples of our fashion: I am therefore sending you several model dolls."

Pandoras—Von Boehn found pandoras were first mentioned in 1642. They were smaller

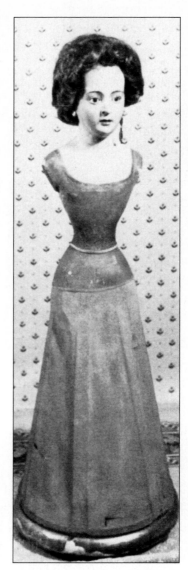

Very early pandora, or small mannequin, used as courier of French fashions. These are seldom found in this fine condition. Note canvas-covered lower part; under this are slats. Photo courtesy of Marcia Cohen, Cohen Auctions.

mannequins, about 36 inches tall, used to carry fashions from France to England, then to other countries. These mannequins were used to display the fashions and coiffures of the day, in the same way full-sized mannequins had been used earlier.

Mannequins and pandoras were no longer needed after 1770, when fashion journals were introduced. However, use of the dolls did not stop immediately. They were still shipped to many countries, and many had complete trousseaus.

When pandoras were being used, they even reached America. The July 2, 1733, edition of the

---

Right: Doll marked *Rohmer*, with painted eyes, is rough white bisque. Unpierced ears are flat. Eye painting is similar to doll marked *Huret* with heavy black line over eyes and eyelashes. Hat is masterpiece of old ribbed silk decorated with faded rose flowers and feathers. It is round in the back and peaks in front. Dolls like this are collected more for historic value than beauty. Doll is shown in full costume on page 105.

the *New England Weekly Journal* ran the following advertisement:

"At Mrs. Hannah Teatts, dressmaker at the top of Summer Street, Boston, is to be seen a mannequin (doll) in the latest fashion, with articles of dress, nightdress and everything appertaining to women's attire. It has been brought from London by Captain White. Ladies who choose to see it may come or send for it. It is always ready to serve you. If you come, it will cost you 2 shillings, but if you send for it, 7 shillings."

There is no description of the doll, but we believe it was a pandora.

Early mannequins were made of wood, papier-mâché or wax. Today, at New England flea markets and estate sales, a mannequinlike doll can occasionally be found. The doll is papier-mâché and modeled only to the waist. It does not have legs but has slats in a circular form to display the skirts to the fullest advantage. Some of the dolls we have seen do not have hair—their wigs were probably detachable to demonstrate current hair fashions. Arms were made so they could be detached for easy costuming. These dolls are about 36 inches tall. The forms are rare today and may be all that remain of early pandoras. See page 10 for a black-and-white photo of one of these forms.

Pandoras were called *great pandoras* (30 to 36 inches tall) and *small pandoras*, to indicate their size. Smaller ones represented children and could be any size under 30 inches.

Paper Dolls—At the end of the 18th century, the English developed something new—the one-sided figure that could be cut out. The figure had many different garments and changeable costumes. The French were quick to adopt its use. They adopted the new idea—the paper doll—as an inexpensive way to advertise Paris fashions. These fashion plates were intended to be cut out and put together like paper dolls.

With fashion plates in magazines, paper dolls, and improvements in communication and transportation, there was not as much use for the full-sized mannequins, which were expensive to dress and ship. Even the pandoras (the half-sized dolls) were not as popular.

PRODUCTION OF PORCELAIN

The Meissen factory began producing porcelain in 1710. The first china doll heads were produced around 1750. They were lady-type heads with gracefully modeled hands. Heads were marked with crossed swords or the letters *K.P.M.*

About 100 years later, around 1850, the use of unglazed heads (bisque) came into use. By this time, porcelain factories were established in most European countries.

Bisque porcelain was beautiful and natural looking, and use of it for doll heads quickly spread. Bisque did not completely replace china or papier-mâché heads, but it became so popular the doll industry grew at a rapid rate.

The new bisque-headed doll began to replace mannequins and pandoras. Bisque dolls were less-expensive to send abroad as fashion couriers. At the same time, French doll-making companies began producing the same ladylike dolls as toys and play dolls.

Von Boehn wrote that around 1850 Natalis Rondo of Paris prepared a report for the French Exposition. In the report, Rondo stated, "Thus these dolls are not only dispatched into the provinces and abroad as samples of fashion; they have become indispensable for the general export of fashionable novelties, for it has been realized that without the aid of the dolls the trade people do not know how to sell their goods."

Today, when we study these bisque-headed dolls with ladylike bodies, we find most are between 6 inches and 16 inches in size. A smaller number are between 20 inches and 30 inches, and a very few are found between 36 inches and 40 inches.

We cannot believe larger lady dolls between 30 and 40 inches (perhaps we can say pandoras) were ever made as toys. The majority of these large dolls that have survived are found in museums dressed as they were originally. No one would accuse the French doll-making industry of such poor judgment as to make a 36-inch lady doll as a child's toy.

Von Boehn also discovered that Jumeau advertised, "The most expensive dolls were those sent to England, Spain and Germany every

---

Right: Old pale-bisque shoulder head. Head has no pate or opening; it is bald. Doll has old, flat cobalt-blue eyes. Holes in lower front and back are called *sew holes,* but heads were seldom sewn on.

Fully articulated, Gesland wood-bodied doll with Gaultier head. She plays harp with alpine flowers around her. Hand-woven red-wool dress has train and is decorated with black and white braid. Underpetticoat has full train.

Pair of Lenore Thomas well-costumed fashion dolls. Hats and accessories add touch of authenticity. Doll on right in tan and green is all original. Doll on left wears reproduction gown copied from fashion plate.

year as fashion models. They are fully dressed at the Jumeau warehouse in the rue Pastourille." This proves Jumeau made fashion dolls as fashion models.

In two editions of Kim McKim's *Doll Talk* (August, 1963 and February, 1971) we found some interesting information. In one edition, an article stated, "By Jumeau's time, French clothes were again highly popular at the London Crystal Palace. In 1851, he took the top medal—for doll clothes!"

Many doll writers today hedge a bit when describing later French fashion dolls by adding *so-called* to their description. We admit the subject is complicated and interwoven with the best products (the dolls themselves) of the golden

age of French dolls, from 1860 to 1890. Fashion dolls are called *French fashions, dressmaker dolls, lady types* and *style dolls*, which indicates emphasis on costumes and accessories. After all, the French were interested in "le femme" (the lady), and from DuBarry to the present, they perfumed, jeweled and dressed their dolls to a king's taste!

French fashion dolls reflected the best of the salons, and entire streets in Paris had busy shops that produced mannequins and trunks of many costume changes. The dolls and their trousseaus helped sell current styles and were also sought for their appeal to young ladies.

A thumbnail description included in *Doll Talk* pictures an exquisite lady doll with elabo-

Left: Marked Huret doll, 16-1/2 inches tall. Swivel head is on shoulderplate. Body is blown leather. This is rare, important doll because few were made. Antique purple-striped silk costume was designed by Marshall Martin in style of costume worn by very early dolls. She wears antique bonnet and side-gusseted, heeled boots. Striped stockings are typical of early period. Underclothing is handsewn. Doll is also shown on page 84.

rately coiffured blond hair. Her beautiful, ruffled silk gown had the necessary accessories of her very feminine era. She had a tiny wasp waist, full hips and full bust—all necessary to carry the fashions of the day. Lady dolls have distinctive proportions of head and body. This was typical of these elaborate dolls.

While Jumeau never seemed to acknowledge his fashion dolls, called *Poupée Parisienne*, he may have been one of the chief producers of these dolls until he became absorbed in his Bébé Jumeau line. The Jumeau stamp is found on some fashion bodies.

Defining the Terms—The terms *fashion doll* or *French fashion doll* are generally used by collectors to describe a particular series of French-made dolls, from Paris, that were made between 1860 and 1900.

Most doll authorities point out these are not true fashion dolls. Clara Fawcett, in her book *Dolls—A New Guide for Collectors* (book is out of print), points out that while the term "fashion doll" is generally used, it is confusing because these bisque lady dolls should be called *Parisiennes*.

Because fashions when the toys/dolls were made were elaborate, collectors have come to call them *fashion dolls*, confusing them with the earlier dolls made as couriers of fashion.

In Colemans' *The Collectors' Encyclopedia of Dolls*, published by Crown in 1968, the same thing is pointed out. They state there is ample evidence the "so-called French fashion dolls" were play dolls and seldom used primarily to display fashionable attire. As proof, they offer the fact that when found in original boxes, these dolls sometimes had no clothing except perhaps a string of beads, a necklace and a ribbon in their hair. So, according to the Colemans, while they are fashion dolls, the name refers not to a doll type but a functional use of dolls.

Most dolls used to display fashions were made much earlier than 1860. Still the term "fashion doll" is generally accepted. It is the misnamed, but ever-popular, French fashion lady or Parisienne of the 1860s and later with which we deal.

In a 1910 edition of an American magazine, *Playthings*, we read, "An old fashion was revived last winter of sending dainty dolls to show the latest Paris fashion."

In studying old advertisements and catalogs, we know fashion-type dolls were sold as toys. Not only were dolls sold but their accessories, trunks and extra costumes were also available. In advertisements, we discovered these dolls were costumed in the finest silks, by unequaled Parisian dressmakers.

Fashion Dolls in Recent Times—In 1949, the French Gratitude Train brought 49 dolls to the United States. One doll was intended for each state and one for the District of Columbia. Today, the dolls are kept together in the costume department of the Brooklyn Museum. They were created by the Syndicate de la Couture de Paris, which included famous costume designers of the time (1940s).

Each doll was dressed in a replica of a costume a well-known person might have worn. Some were costumed as famous ladies, such as Empress Eugenie, the Marquise de Pompadour, Marie Antoinette, Empress Josephine and Empress Elizabeth of Austria. Some dolls were dressed as famous women of paintings by artists Wahtean, Lancret, Winterhalter and Tadema.

The dolls are each 30 inches tall—the same size as original pandoras. Dates of costumes reflect fashions from 1715 to 1906. Each doll shows meticulous artistry in dress, millinery, hairstyle, shoes, gloves and furs. Many collectors consider these costumes to be the finest ever created for dolls.

These gift dolls provide a valuable record of costume and dressmaking artistry and a unique document of the history of French fashion dolls. The 49 dolls were shown in a booklet titled *Two Centuries of French Fashion, An Album of Mannequin Dolls*, published in 1950 by Charles Scribner's Sons, New York. This is the last instance we can find of the use of dolls as couriers of fashion from France.

These dolls were mannequin types (pandoras) with a wire armature in the bodies and composition heads.

Right: 27-inch doll, marked *F.G.* for François Gaultier. Body is all leather. Leather hands and fingers are individually wired so doll can hold something. Toes are indicated with stitching. Blouse is gold brocade-silk, with self-covered buttons. Jacket and skirt are black silk. Ruffle of old lace finishes each sleeve. Black silk ruffles add character to jacket, bottom of full skirt and edge of sleeves. Doll is also shown on page 132.

French fashion dolls make interesting arrangements. Here two dolls play chess. Note proportion of chairs, table and board. Doll in blue is marked *H*, and doll in lavender has twill-covered body with joints in ankle. Lenore Thomas dolls.

Other side of chess table shows wood-bodied doll with ball-joint in waist wearing pale-aqua-silk dress. She has old flat eyes and is marked *F*. Doll in blue-and-white dress has blond-mohair wig and blue eyes. Lenore Thomas dolls.

FRENCH FASHION DOLLS AS TOYS

French fashion dolls made as couriers of Parisian fashions were also made as children's toys. They were made for young girls to dress and undress, to enjoy at tea parties and to take for walks. The dolls, with elaborate trousseaus, trunks and accessories, were similar to today's popular Barbie doll, with her accessories.

Fashion dolls were the toys of rich French children, but many dolls were exported for children of the wealthy in England, the United States and other European countries.

It's easy to prove French fashion dolls were made as toys. Study toy catalogs from 1878 to 1910, and you'll find French fashion dolls with many accessories. They are listed as French dolls, but the illustrations show lady dolls fully costumed—the doll we call the "French fashion doll."

Lithographs in ladies magazines of the 1860s, '70s and '80s, such as *Ehrich's Fashion Quarterly, Godey's Fashions, Delineator, Harper's Young People, Harper's Bazaar* and *Lapoupée Modele* show paintings and sketches of children at play. Girls play with the dolls and dress them up or play tea party with them. Magazines also included patterns for doll costumes.

An 1878 advertisement for Schwarts of Boston showed French fashion dolls in their

---

Left: Doll is marked *F.G.* on head and shoulderplate. She has bright-blue, lined paperweight eyes. Ears are pierced through lobe. Eyelashes are black, and well-painted eyebrows are dark brown. Blond-mohair wig is full. Lips are well-shaped and accented. This head came from very good or unused mold. Note strong, well-formed features. She is shown in full costume on page 8.

Marked Huret doll with smaller twin Heubach dolls. Huret has shoulder head, painted eyes and gray human-hair wig. Dress is well-preserved. White-on-white soutache braid decorates cotton that has stood the test of time. Off-shoulder design was style from 1850 to early 1860s. Lenore Thomas dolls.

Right: Portrait Jumeau is pressed bisque and has applied ears and mauve blush over eyes, which indicates very early doll. Lips are painted in two tones of pompadore. Gray paperweight eyes have dark rim on iris. Eye holes are handcut and not exactly even. Eyebrows are tiny lines in arch, and old wig matches brows. Antique bonnet is red plum-colored velvet. Inside brim is lined with duller plum-colored silk, and flowers are soft pink. Doll is shown without hat on page 78.

"Toy Emporium." Dolls were described as wearing the latest, most-exquisite Parisian styles, with trousseaus. Affluent parents considered these dolls fun and educational for the overindulged young lady. A trunk of clothing and the luxurious accessories a lady doll needed helped instill in a child what it was like to be a lady. At first these dolls were owned only by the children of aristocrats, but by the early 20th century they were also in the possession of children of middle-class parents.

Children of the 1880s were taught to take care of their toys and other possessions. This may be the reason so many lovely French fashion dolls are still available today.

Many doll shops and stalls in and around Paris sold and repaired dolls. Any doll that was played with could be broken, especially when it was made of bisque. These shops replaced heads, hands or feet, as was necessary. This is why today, without any recent tampering, we find strange combinations of heads and bodies. Extra parts were also available, and mothers probably didn't hesitate to put on a new part without being concerned whether a head and body matched.

Doll in all-original, pink-and-white dress has tricolored eyes (expression eyes). Hands are bisque. She has been preserved as part of history by Lenore Thomas.

Left: 21-inch Smiler, also shown on cover, is marked G. Ears are pierced through lobe; she wears one original gold-and-amethyst earring. Body is stuffed leather with individually wired fingers. Couturier-designed costume is made in two shades of lavender silk-taffeta. Jacket is fitted with eight tiny darts. Low, draped shawl collar is filled in with gathered antique lace. Collar is fastened at center front with six-petal flower of same fabric. Jacket closes with seven self-covered buttons and is pointed in back and front with extra fullness at hips. Skirt has three rows of tiny knife pleats; over the skirt are six diagonal pleats. Self-fabric bow is attached at left. Pleats become bustle and train in back. Three-quarter length sleeves are fitted and end with two gathered ruffles of lace. Costume is lined with glazed tan fabric. Hat is woven straw with pale lavender bands, tiny pink and lavender flowers and beaded feathers. Doll wears high boots with heels and carries binoculars and an antique gold-tipped, ivory-handle umbrella. She is also shown on page 116.

The Fabulous Costumes

There are few things in the doll world as interesting or as varied as the bodies of fashion dolls. But the incredible costumes of the Parisiennes may be what first appeal to a new collector, and they can even intrigue advanced collectors.

Parisiennes were made in several colors of bisque to represent different nationalities. We have found dolls of black, brown and yellow bisque, but the majority were white. They were often dressed in costumes according to the country of their destination. See pages 27 and 28.

In addition to beautiful Parisian costumes, dolls were dressed as maids, children's nurses and workers. See page 8. We know of one doll that was dressed as a priest. But these dolls aren't common. Fashion dolls dressed in regional costumes are more common.

Very early Huret and Rohmer dolls, and perhaps others from the 1850-to-1860 period, were often dressed in a midcalf, full-skirted dress of Marseilles cloth, which is ribbed cotton fabric. Dresses were decorated with soutache braid handsewn in designs. There were many designs and color combinations, such as white braid on white, black on white, bright blue on dark blue, red on white, brown on tan and others. Photos show different combinations. See pages 20 and 26.

Horizontally striped stockings were the fad between 1850 and 1860. Some stockings were bright colors, such as lavender, pink or blue. See page 14.

Gowns and Dresses—The most incredible costumes of the Parisiennes were the fantastic ball gowns. We have three in our collection. One has cascades of pale-pink lace and net lined with pink silk-taffeta. See page 38. Another is printed silk-taffeta with layered panels, ribbons and flowers. See page 45. The third gown is white satin stripe on transparent silk. The top and bal-

---

Left: 24-inch doll, marked *E.J.* for Emile Jumeau, has swivel head. Blond wig is mohair. Body is leather, including wired fingers and sewn toes. Hat is antique straw with stone-green satin-ribbon trim. Gown is iridescent stone-green antique taffeta with lace front. Sleeves are fitted and have lace cuffs. She carries lace shawl and antique satin-and-silk umbrella with ivory handle. Doll wears old brown-leather, high-top, high-heeled boots that lace up front. She is also shown on page 7.

Gutta-percha body by Huret with 1860 costume of white cotton trimmed with red soutache braid. Undyed sheepskin wig is extra-long.

Fine antique hat was woven of hair, probably horsehair. Crown is tied with ribbon and tiny flowers. Doll is also shown on page 127.

Fitted and wired black velvet hat with big black feather on head of Smiler marked 1. Doll is also shown on page 42.

looned back are cranberry velvet. See page 30.

We have found dolls dressed in walking dresses, tea dresses, dinner dresses, morning dresses and occasionally a child's dress. See page 6. There was a dress for every time of day, every occasion and in every kind of fabric. Most costumes were elaborately decorated and made with the expertise of a couturier.

Outdoor Clothing—Outdoor clothing was also stylish. Many extras, such as muffs, fur pieces, shawls and boots, came in a trunk. We have also found an original wool coat-style dress with a fur piece, hat and muff to match. See pages 32 and 142. One lady doll, dressed in dark-green satin, also has a dark-green velvet cape edged in mink and a mink muff. Her hat is dark-green velvet. See page 30.

Sometimes there is seasonal clothing for dolls. We even found record of a bathing suit.

Hats—Most fashion dolls wore hats. Like wigs, hats were played with and often changed from one doll to another. Hats are best shown in pictures. See the pictures on this page and the following pages. When looking at hats, envision unfaded flowers and bright ribbons.

Right: Perfectly preserved doll dressed in regional finery. This is one of a pair of French fashion dolls labeled *Brittany Wedding, 1869*. Handmade, hand-embroidered costume is color-coordinated. Note balance of beige, red and black colors. Second doll is shown on page 28.

Turned-up straw hat with folded cocoa-brown band and cocoa-colored feather matches costume colors. Lenore Thomas doll.

Double-ruffled bonnet often worn under hooded capes. It is found on early dolls, usually Hurets from 1850 to 1860.

Soft black-velvet cap, trimmed with coral velvet and black feathers.

Wired bonnet stitched with gold and black velvet. This is shaped head piece.

Left: Lady doll is dressed in costume of fine wool. This 27-inch doll has shoulder head, old cobalt-blue eyes and full leather body. Dolls of this quality are good investments.

Green velvet shaped hat with black-feather trim.

Variety of shoes for French fashion dolls.

Shoes and Boots—Shoes, boots and slippers were worn by French fashion dolls. They were made with or without heels and were usually leather. Study the styles in the photo above. Shoes may also have been changed from one doll to another.

TYPES OF COSTUMES

There are three types of *original* costumes found on lady dolls, and it is not difficult to distinguish between them. After studying the different types of original costumes, you may find it easier to recognize a reproduction costume. A contemporary costume is not as easy to recognize. We discuss the different types of costumes so you will know what you are buying.

Couturier Fashions—Costumes were designed and made by a special costumer for one doll.

They are the most sought after by collectors of French fashion dolls. Costumes are the ultimate in design and workmanship and were made entirely by hand.

Outfits are completely lined and made of the finest fabrics. You can easily recognize pleating and draping done by a professional. Study finishing inside each garment.

Lady dolls wearing these fine costumes are the most desired *and* the most difficult to find. The fine silks and silk-taffetas quickly deteriorated and disintegrated. When found, these costumes are often in a sad state of repair. Only costumes that have been carefully protected have survived.

One small detail in costuming we have found is *pinking*. Pinking was used as a finish on decorations of original fashions done by couturiers. It made finer cuts than pinking shears used today.

Right: Rohmer doll wears elaborate winter ball gown. Jacket, bustle and train are cranberry velvet trimmed with gold-embroidered silk lace over ruching. Front panel of dress is transparent silk with horizontal satin stripes. Side and back of dress are white silk with vertical black stripes and brocade flowers. Dress is finished at bottom with delicate black-edged net and drawstring ribbons. Hat is made in shape and color of two pansies and edged to match dress.

Hand-colored Godey's fashions taken from original *Ladies' Friend Magazine* published in 1864.

Use these authentic fashion plates to design gowns for your dolls. From 1870 *Ladies' Friend Magazine.*

In June, 1874, *Peterson's Magazine* included this hand-colored engraving.

We purchased *Ladies' Friend Magazine* (1865 to 1875) from doll museum. These hand-painted water-colored prints from stone engravings may help you as a costumer.

Commercially Made Fashions—These costumes were sewn by machine, and many were probably made exactly alike for a production line of dolls. These costumes are more apt to be found on later dolls that were made when French doll-making companies were trying to economize. Commercially made costumes are valuable because they are a part of history.

Commercial costumes were usually fully lined but were not made of the finest fabrics. Decorations were somewhat gaudy or overdone instead of the more subtle, well-planned decorations of couturier-made fashions.

Upon close inspection, you will probably find anything that is covered on these costumes is unfinished, such as the top of the skirt, the top of underdrawers or any other garment edge that did not show.

Left: Unmarked doll in winter costume is pressed bisque. She has unpierced ears. Eyebrows are thin, dark-brown lines, and eyelashes are charcoal. Deep-blue paperweight eyes enhance her face. Hat, which is stiff and wired around brim, is made of black velvet and trimmed with brown and plum ribbon to match costume. Doll is also shown on page 142.

Les modes du siècle

1826   1830   1835

1851   1855   1860

1876   1880   1885

Use these sketches to help you match time of your costumes and dolls. Reproduced with permission of François Theimer, editor of *Polichinelle,* a French doll magazine.

1840   1845   1850

1865   1870   1875

1890   1895   1899

Doll dressed in purple-and-cream striped cotton; braid fringe was added as decoration. Costume is old, perhaps mother-made. Doll wears antique underclothing.

Unusual doll with long face and large, uneven eyes. Owner thinks it may have been made by Lanternier. Doll is dressed in reproduction costume of cotton. Lenore Thomas doll.

Homemade Fashions—The third type of costume for a lady doll was the homemade or mother-made dress. These varied more in type, construction and material than couturier or commercially made costumes. Sewing could be wonderful or terrible, depending on the time and skill of the person dressing the doll.

Homemade costumes often represented everyday dresses, work dresses or simple afternoon dresses. They were usually made from materials at hand, such as pieces left from an adult costume or fabric from a worn-out garment. Sometimes fabric was not suitable for a doll.

In rare instances, a doll's head was the only piece purchased, and the costume *and* body were made at home. This practice was more common with German dolls than French dolls.

Contemporary Costumes—A contemporary costume was made about the same time as a doll but not *for* her. These costumes can usually be determined by fit. A costume made for the doll will fit around the waist and at the shoulders, and it is the correct length. If the dress fits well and is of the correct date, don't be concerned.

Reproduction Outfits—Reproduction costumes are easy to recognize. Few doll costumers have the skill of French seamstresses of 100 years ago. To determine if a costume is a reproduction, check overall appearance. If it is old, a costume *must* be faded. Check the back and where fabric laps inside. Check lining, and examine inside finishing. Modern fabrics are usually distinguishable. Is the costume handsewn? Does the dress look too new and too perfect? If it does, it may be a reproduction dress.

Look underneath to see if underclothing is old and the body is unworn. If a doll was unplayed with, this might account for her perfection.

Right: Unmarked 14-inch swivel-head doll is on Gesland body. She has well-modeled bisque feet and hands. Swivel head is pale bisque. She wears English reproduction dress of antique blue silk trimmed with unusual lace edging. Dress is in three parts—full skirt, jacket and white cotton blouse.

Dolls that have reproduction costumes are usually dolls that were played with, and wear will show on the body.

Reproduction costumes of old fabrics, made by modern couturiers, are more difficult to recognize. Check the thread to see if it is silk or polyester. Sometimes modern lace is added to old fabrics, and this may lead you to believe the entire costume is a reproduction. Sometimes the style itself will tell you a costume is a reproduction.

When collecting lady dolls, you may want a representation of each type of costume. If you only want lady dolls with original couturier costumes, it will limit your collection, and you will lose the joy of variety. Think of fashion dolls first as bits of history, then as toys that may have had their costumes changed.

Don't be upset if a dealer sells you a doll stating, "It's all original," but when you get it home, you determine it isn't. Did the costume look original when you bought it?

Doll collecting is a gamble, no matter how you do it, and we *all* take some chances. But there are some things you can do to protect yourself. Deal with reputable dealers. Refuse to do business with a dealer if he or she misrepresents a doll. Tell your friends of your experiences—you'll help all collectors and help make the doll world better.

Portrait Jumeau wearing morning apron and inside bonnet (bonnet worn before hair was arranged in the morning). Doll is 28 inches tall on kid body. Doll is also shown on page 80.

FABRICS AND COLORS

In this period of French fashions, all fabrics were made from natural materials. Basically four materials were used—silk, wool, cotton and linen. From these four, many combinations, different weaves and interesting textures were created. A beautiful range of colors was available from natural and chemical dyes.

Fabrics—Silk included French silk, Japanese silk, weighted silk (mineral salts were added to give it weight), silk-taffeta, failles, iridescent silks, silk-brocades, satins, velvets and many others. Wools included soft, fine challis, flannel, cashmere and nobby wools for coats.

Cottons ranged from fine batiste to heavy, colorful velvets. Cotton prints were also available. White cotton was usually used for underclothes, with the exception of wool-flannel petticoats. Linen was made in different weights and weaves. Plaids were woven of combinations of materials.

Trims—Doll couturiers lavishly trimmed each costume as if it were a masterpiece. They used festoons (garlands of flowers), scallops, pleating, ruching (tiny pleating) and tatting (type of edge trim). They also used rosettes, frills, feathers, flowers, braid and fringe, in addition to ribbons, laces, buttons and beads. The sewing machine was used but not for fine finishes on costumes.

Colors—Dressmakers used many colors and combinations of colors. Indigo was grown for the sole purpose of making blue dye. From indigo, the dressmaker used fabrics dyed bright blue, powder blue, sapphire, peacock, dusty blue, pale blue, deep violet, plum, grape and mauve.

Left: Leather-bodied Jumeau doll wears elaborate pink-net ball gown, lined with pink satin and underfabric of silk-taffeta. Top is pink silk-taffeta with ruffles. Full skirt and train have cascading lace and ruffles, lined with inset lace, and tiny silk flowers. Doll is 17 inches tall and marked 3.

Original three-quarter-length chemise, drawers and corset.

Back view of Jumeau doll wearing original chemise.

Corset, drawers and petticoat.

White was basic and shaded into cream, ivory, natural and beige. Tones and shades of brown were used, as were earth colors and deep cinnamon or chocolate.

Red tinted to pink and cranberry. Soft, muted greens, stone green, mint green, apple green and emerald green were used less frequently, but they were used.

The palette of colors used on fashion dolls has an effect on collectors. Often it is the color combination of the beautiful garments that first appeals to a collector.

When costuming French fashion dolls, it is the shades and tones of colors that make the task a joy. And the colors make the study and photography of fashion dolls enjoyable.

UNDERCLOTHING

The style of undergarments worn by Parisiennes changed little during the 60 years of the dolls' popularity. Undergarments were made of cotton—from the finest batiste to coarse muslin.

A few undergarments were made of fine linen. All were white. The only exception we have found was outer petticoats, which occasionally were red, blue or cream wool flannel.

A doll usually wore three undergarments—a chemise, underdrawers and a petticoat. A doll might wear as many as three petticoats at the same time.

Cotton garments were lavishly trimmed with lace, tatting and embroidery. Seamstresses often used embroidery stitches as decoration around the bottom of flannel petticoats. Sometimes crocheted lace was used.

Dolls found in "original condition" usually have matching underclothes. All underclothing of a doll was made of the same material and trimmed with the same lace.

In addition to a chemise, underdrawers and a petticoat, we sometimes find a fashion doll with a corset. See photos above. We have also found wire hoops used to hold out full skirts. See page 122.

Right: 16-inch articulated wood-bodied doll displays her elaborate petticoat with train. Petticoat is decorated with fine eyelet and rows of tiny handsewn tucks. She also has wire hoops and corset. Chemise is three-quarter-length. Underclothing fills out and improves costume's appearance. Steiner child doll is looking into hand mirror that came in larger doll's trunk.

Examining the Bodies of French Fashion Dolls

The study of the bodies of French fashion dolls can be complete in itself. Bodies were made of many different materials, with different joint arrangements. In this section, we include photos to help you see what you might never see—the incredible variations in the number of unusual bodies we have found. Body photos follow the general discussion below.

KID AND LEATHER BODIES

The most-common body found on French fashion dolls is the kid or leather body. The body is kid or leather, including torso, legs, feet, arms and hands, and is often handsewn.

The body has a slender waist and full hips. Often a bosom was formed by inserting cotton under the top of the leather. Some bodies had mittenlike hands, with stitching to indicate fingers. Other bodies had hands with individually stitched fingers and wire in each finger. Feet didn't usually have toes, but some dolls had stitching to indicate toes.

There are many French fashion dolls available today with leather or kid bodies. The majority, perhaps as many as 80% of those on the market, have an all-kid body. There are other bodies, but they are rare and expensive.

WOOD BODIES

The finely crafted wood body with joints in the wrist, ankle and waist is most desired by collectors. Another wood body has a second joint to twist arms or legs into many positions. Other articulated wood bodies were covered with wet kid that shrank as it dried. A rare wood body covered with twill is usually found only in museums.

The articulated wood body of a fashion doll has stood the test of time far better than cloth, leather or kid doll bodies. And it is a masterpiece of craftsmanship.

BLOWN-LEATHER BODIES

One of the rarest leather fashion bodies was the *blown-leather body*—the body was completely empty. Hands, with separate fingers, and feet were also empty leather.

GUTTA-PERCHA BODIES

Another rare body was made of gutta-percha,

Left: Leather-bodied 18-inch Smiler was re-dressed in red silk and black lace 45 years ago when she was added to a museum. Top was created by gathering and puffing material. Feathered hat matches dress.

a rubberlike substance. A few of these bodies can still be found.

CLOTH BODIES

Many cloth bodies were also made. These included factory-made bodies, homemade ones and a very special body made of metal armatures that were padded and covered with stockinette. The armature was usually padded with cotton so it was firm; then stockinette was sewn tightly over the form. Some of these bodies are still in fine shape. They were made by Gesland and usually have bisque hands and feet.

LEARNING ABOUT BODIES

There are endless combinations of body materials, including leather, kid, bisque, china, cloth and wood. Bodies were solid, unstuffed or stuffed with cotton, wool, hair, seaweed, cork, sawdust or bran.

One doll with a kid body has no leg joints or hip joints. The body is stuffed so tightly she stands alone. Metal pegs mounted on her wood stand fit into the holes in the soles of her feet to hold her upright. See page 72. Another late fashion doll, made by Limoges, had metal feet, a cloth body and bisque hands. It is important to understand that in some cases heads could have been changed from the original body to another body.

Generally, the oldest of these shapely doll bodies exhibit the finest craftsmanship and ingenuity. For instance, ball-joints similar to those used in wood-bodied French fashions were used on dolls *before* 1850. Some of the earliest producers of the lady-type doll—Marie Rohmer, Calixte Huret, Marie Bruchet and Benoit Martin—made doll bodies with ingenious joints.

The photos of the bodies, mainly from dolls in our collection, show many materials and variations. Study them so you will know how to select French fashion dolls. They will also help you understand which bodies will bring higher prices.

Sometimes the seams of leather fashion bodies can help you identify the maker of a particular body. For instance, if one body is marked and another is sewn exactly like it, even though the body is bigger or smaller, chances are it was made in the same factory. There are usually three hip seams. Some seams have kid piping for reinforcement.

One body, marked *D'AUTREMONT, Paris, 8 Rue Du Dauphine*, has a V of piping from the hips to the crotch on the front and gussets in the knees and hips. Arms and hands on the doll are china; the china arm stops above the elbow.

The marked Rohmer body has one seam from crotch to chest on the front and three seams on the back. This body sometimes has two grommets (eyelets) on the front. Ribbons protruding from the eyelets could be used to tie legs in a sitting position. Ribbons were attached to the inside of the arm; when pulled, they bent the arm up. We have not seen another doll with ribbons attached in this way. See page 65.

The Smiler head is usually found on a leather body with a seam that goes down around the slightly protruding tummy. Body has knee gussets, hip gussets and three hip seams. (For more information on Smilers, see page 90.) This body exactly matches one marked *Bru Breveté* body, so we can assume the body and head are by Bru.

There is another variation of the front tummy seam that is piped with kid. This is the Y-form. Two seams come from hips in front to meet one seam coming from the crotch. Hip, knee and elbow gussets are also used on this body. We have found this several times on dolls marked *EB* (probably for Barrois). We found the same body, without piping but with handsewn seams, on dolls stamped *Guiton* and *Simonne*.

Sometimes it helps to match bodies or head markings or to compare sizes of different dolls. Occasionally, studying face painting on a doll will help identify it.

Another rare body that is seldom seen is a metal body covered with kid. Lower arms and hands are brass. Kid over the upper torso is drawn tight, and the lower back is left loose for movement or sitting. Lower legs are wood. This body has also been found with china hands and legs. There are no markings on the body.

Right: Tiny fashion doll with body marked *Guiton*. Her pixie expression is different from most fashions. Doll wears beautiful handsewn costume. Dress fabric is delicate, cream-colored silk-taffeta with green stripes and pink roses. Coat is fitted and bound with same fabric. Train has gathered decorator lace around bottom. Above this, another edging of delicate lace is laced with ribbon. Under it is ruffle of pale-green taffeta. Upper skirt is drawn into bustle and sewn with lace and soft, faded flowers. Bustle extends down back in five separate, lace-edged panels. Pieces of pale-green velvet ribbon are also used. Ruffles of lace and embroidered lace are matched on hat and neck. Doll has all-leather body.

Fully articulated, wood-bodied doll marked 2.

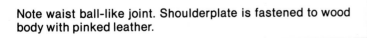

Note waist ball-like joint. Shoulderplate is fastened to wood body with pinked leather.

WOOD-BODIED DOLL NO. 2

This doll body can be identified because she is on a body attributed to Gesland. The shape of the face exactly matches the face of F.G. dolls. She is 18 inches tall.

Her wood body has a pleasant, ladylike shape without a bosom. Shoulder joints have a peg swivel and a tongue-and-groove joint. There is an added joint, called a *twist joint,* in the middle of the upper arm that allows the arm to turn. Hands have a ball-joint in a socket.

Upper legs are attached to an oval in the front of the hips. The upper leg moves forward on a tongue-and-groove joint. An additional twist joint is used in each upper leg, which allows the doll to sit with legs crossed. The knee joint only moves forward and backward. Legs and feet are solid wood.

The head has the appearance of an F.G. head but is marked only with a 4. The shoulderplate is attached to the wood torso with a glued-on piece of kid. Wood joints are held in place with many wood pegs.

The body is painted with pale-wheat-colored enamel. It is almost the same color as the doll's sheepskin wig. The fur of the wig is long and hangs in a tangle down her back.

One big toe is missing on one foot, and all the toes are missing on the other foot. This doll was purchased from an English doll dealer at a United Federation of Doll Clubs (UFDC) Convention in San Antonio, Texas, in 1984. We bought the doll dressed and were not told of these defects, but the price reflected her damage.

Details of face modeling are not as strong as they could be. This head looks as if it came from a well-used mold. (For additional information on how French dolls were made 100 years ago, read our book *How to Collect French Bébé Dolls,* also published by HPBooks.)

Eyebrows are very thin; the artist used fine strokes of the pen. Eyes are lined in charcoal, and eyelashes are the same color. Paperweight eyes are light blue, with a deeper blue rim around the iris.

Ears were made in the mold and are pierced through the lobe.

This lady doll came with a wool gown, cape and hat. She had a petticoat but no underdrawers. The doll also had a few small items from what we assume was her original trunk, including a handbag, brush, mirror and clothes brush.

VARIATIONS

One variation of this type of wood body has additional twist joints in the upper legs and waist. The torso, a small section of the upper leg and the upper arms have leather shrunk over them. Joints are covered in the hips but are not worn in the shoulders. Bisque arms, tinted fingers and shoulder head all appear to be Rohmer, but a body with twist joints is usually attributed to Gesland.

A second variation on the all-wood Gesland body is a body with a waist joint and rather large, round hips. Wood Gesland bodies usually have twist joints, but this one has these joints only in the upper leg. Knee joints are a carved ball, the same as the shoulder joints. Head is marked 4 and *F.G.*

A third interesting variation is the one with the blue oval *Simonne* stamp. She is 17 inches tall. Her shoulder head is attached to her wood torso by a strip of leather. Shoulder joints are wood, covered with kid. Lower arms are bisque and are similar to arms on Rohmer dolls. Solid-wood legs and feet have tongue-and-groove joints. Toes are carved into the wood.

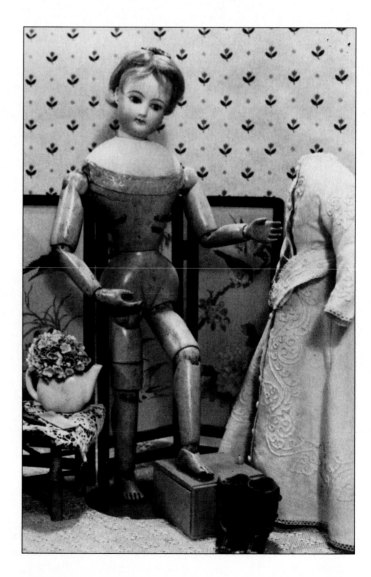

Unusual wood body made by Gesland. Note carved fingers, wrist joints, carved toes and ankle joints. Marcia Cohen, of Cohen Auctions, called our attention to this doll.

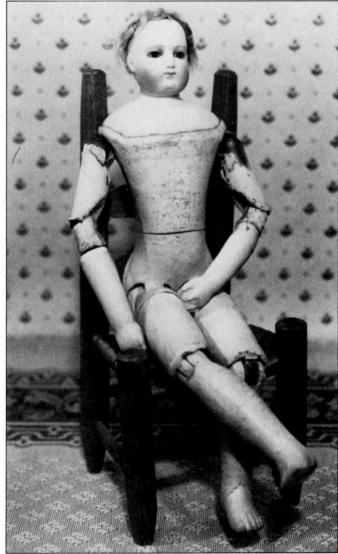

Shoulder-head doll has blue paperweight eyes on fine wood body stamped *Simonne.* Arms and head appear to be Rohmer. This is good investment doll. Photo courtesy Cohen Auctions.

Rare Gesland body with waist swivel and upper-leg swivel. Compare this with wood body not covered with leather. Photo courtesy Cohen Auctions.

WOOD-BODIED DOLL NO. 3

The head of this doll has no number or marking, but we have three clues to her identity—the shape of her face, her wood body covered with leather and shoes marked with a keystone. (*Leather* is tanned animal skin and thicker than kid. *Kid* is animal skin that has been thinned by scraping or splitting. Both types of coverings were used.)

This type of body is usually attributed to Jumeau. The keystone on the boots and the face shape are attributed to Bru. The doll remains unidentified because boots could have been changed, and the body may have been made by one of several doll companies. She is 18-1/2 inches tall.

The wood body is covered with kid, including the joints. Wet kid was applied to the wood. It shrank as it dried and fit like skin. Upper arms and upper legs are wood and covered with kid. Lower arms are bisque, with an added wood joint. Lower legs are sawdust-stuffed kid with added wood joints.

The shoulder has a swivel joint and a tongue-and-groove joint; movement is similar to the movement of a human shoulder. Elbow joints are tongue-and-groove. There is no joint in the wrist because hands are bisque to the midforearm, where they are attached to leather-covered wood that goes into the upper-arm-elbow joint.

Hips are tongue-and-groove joints, which move easily. Knees are also tongue-and-groove joints, and each is covered with leather. The foot, with five sewn toes, and the lower leg are stuffed with sawdust. The toe and bottom of the foot are separate pieces of leather. Seams are handsewn.

This doll's face has the roundness and double chin of early dolls. Ears were made in the mold and are unpierced.

Note the doll's "collar" shoulderplate. Her swivel head is delicately painted, and bisque is smooth. Her eyebrows are pale-wheat color and painted with fine strokes. Eyes are deep-blue paperweight.

This doll came in an antique box that was probably hers. Her original dress is plum-colored wool, decorated with fringe and black-velvet trim. She has a fur piece, muff and hat. Her underclothing consists of petticoat, underdrawers, corset, chemise and stockings.

WOOD-BODIED DOLL NO. 4

These two dolls are a marked Rohmer and an unmarked Rohmer—they have identical heads. Note "washer-woman" arm and hands with elbow on doll on right. Doll kneeling in chair has wood body covered with leather. Leather body of doll on right is stuffed with some type of hair—her body is described under Leather-Bodied Doll No. 1, page 64.

The leather-covered wood body of the doll kneeling in the chair has a few handsewn seams. The rest of the leather of the body was applied wet, and it shrank as it dried to fit the wood form.

Sturdy tongue-and-groove hip joints allow the doll to sit. Knee joints are the same type. Legs below the knee are bisque, with well-modeled toes.

Arms are double-jointed at the shoulder with a swivel joint and a tongue-and-groove joint. The elbow has the same joint as the knees. Arms and type are bisque and are heavy "washer-woman" hands found on many Rohmer dolls.

The pressed swivel head and shoulderplate are pale bisque. There are almost no ears.

The doll's face is well-painted. Her blue-glass eyes are flat.

This doll was repaired at Emma Clear's Humpty Dumpty Doll Hospital in the 1930s. Note the screws added in the shoulder joint where wood pegs were used originally. Fingers on the left hand have also been repaired.

The doll was fully dressed when we bought her. Her second petticoat was full in the back with a train. Drawers are the split type. Her dress, which was made of silk-brocade, has deteriorated, and there is little left of it. Her black-heeled shoes are slipper-style.

WOOD-BODIED DOLL NO. 5—PHENIX

This Phenix body of wood, with its unusual joints, is an extremely rare one. The doll belongs to Lenore Thomas. On the front of the body is a brass oval label *Bte S.G.D.G., La Poupée, Phenix, Marque Déposé.* See page 95.

The doll is jointed at the knees, elbows and shoulders. Shoulders have two different joints so they can turn sideways and be raised or lowered. Elbow and knee joints can swivel, and they move forward and backward. The most unusual joint is in the hips. They are separate from the waist, and the entire hip rotates to make a very natural-looking body.

There is a screw in the center side of the hip. The rest of the body is put together with wood pegs, except the hands, which are hollow metal. A metal band around the wrist appears to be held together with rivets.

Each lower leg and foot is a solid piece of wood. Toes and arches are carved, and toenails are indicated.

This body is the same as the rare body marked *Martin*, except the Martin body has joints in the ankles.

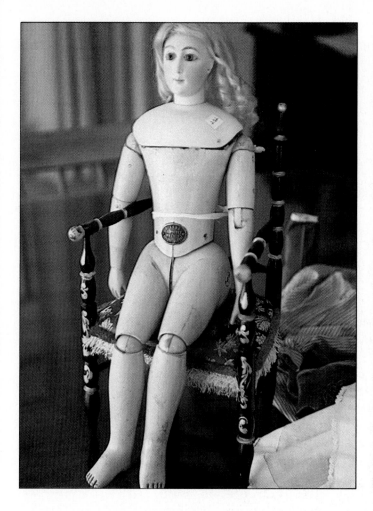

Above: Phenix body is masterpiece of craftsmanship. Lenore Thomas doll.

Above right: This may be only body like this in existence.

Right: Study joints and humanlike movement they provide.

TWILL-COVERED,
WOOD-BODIED DOLL NO. 6

There are no marks on the head or shoulderplate of this rare, well-preserved fashion doll. Her bisque head was pressed. She stands 16 inches tall.

The body, including feet, are covered with silk-twill. Bisque arms below the elbow are the only exception. Twill was stretched and glued over the wood pieces until it fit like skin. It was even put over the tongue of the joints in the hips, knees and ankles.

This doll is in mint condition. Her body is unsoiled, as if it had always been covered. Joints are similar to the well-jointed wood bodies of Jumeau dolls. The circular movement in the shoulders is achieved with a connecting rod or mortise-and-tenon joint. A second joint lets the arm move up and down. Hip joints are tongue-and-groove, with a metal pin going through the hips. Knees are tongue-and-groove, but the casing of the upper leg covers them. Ankle joints are tongue-and-groove with leg casing covering the joint. A metal pin in the ankle facilitates movement. Toes are indicated where twill is pressed over the carved wood.

Lovely tinted-bisque hands are posed in a graceful position. Nails are deeply impressed and also tinted.

The modeling of the nose and lips is superb, and painting is delicate. The bulging, pale-blue paperweight eyes are spectacular. Eyebrows are feathered to perfection.

Ears are pierced into the head.

LEATHER-COVERED,
WOOD-BODIED DOLL NO. 7

The head of this doll is marked *1:*, and the shoulder is marked *J*. The two dots with the 1 are deeply embedded in the bisque. This doll has been in our possession for a long time. She was sold to us as a Jumeau, which we believe she is. There is some question about calling the *J* a positive Jumeau identification. We know Jumeau used *numbers* for sizes. This doll is 14 inches tall.

The wood torso is pleasantly shaped and covered with wet-shrunk leather. All seams are handsewn. Upper and lower legs are completely covered with leather, with a single seam down the back. Feet are also leather-covered. Toes are indicated by a line of stitching. The leather toe section and a leather piece for the sole were added to the foot.

The shoulder has a swivel joint and a joint made of a flat, circular piece of wood that is 1/4 inch thick. The arm has a groove that fits over the circular wood piece. A wood pin passes down through the circular piece of wood to allow the arm to move easily. This is an improvement over the tongue-and-groove joint used in other dolls.

Arms and hands are wood and painted cream color. The hand is well-shaped, and nails are carved in. The elbow joint is the same as the shoulder joint. Hip joints have a metal disk for movement. Knee joints are completely covered by the upper leg section and move on a metal disk.

Her shoulderplate has two sew holes in front and two in back. The hollow for the swivel head is lined with thin kid.

Eyelashes are charcoal. Her deep-gold-colored eyebrows are painted with run-together strokes. Her gray paperweight eyes are circled with black.

This doll has very large, well-designed ears, which are pierced through the lobe.

She wears her original gold-blond mohair wig in an interesting style. It is pinned in place with gold hairpins. One of her earrings is gold, and the other is a replacement.

She has a chemise, split drawers, corset, petticoat and a second petticoat with extra material and fullness in back.

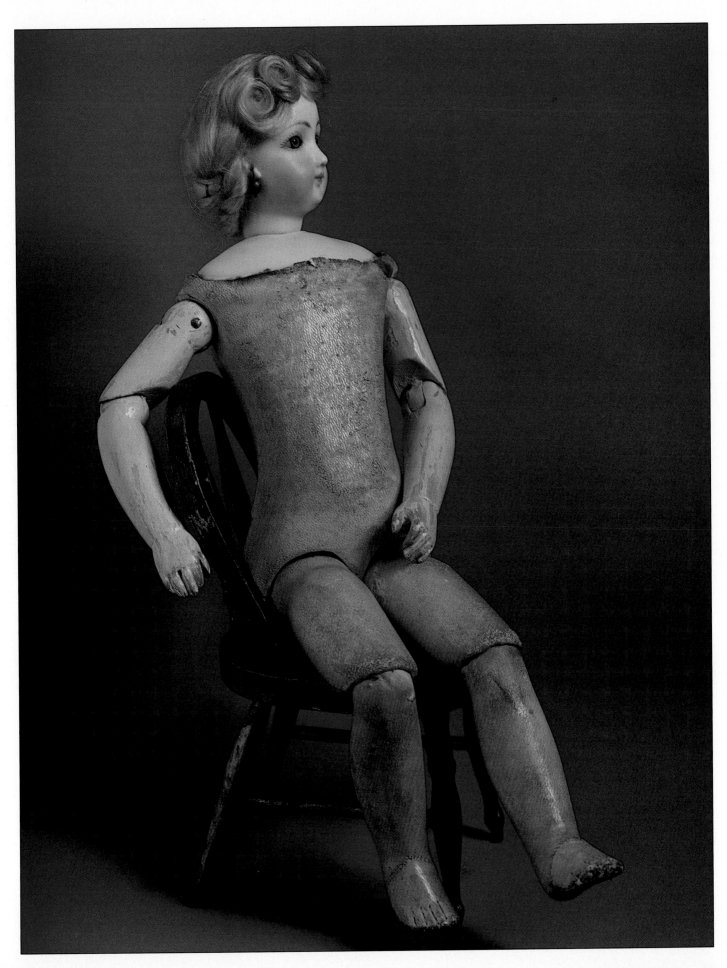

BLOWN-LEATHER-BODIED DOLL

The 17-inch doll on the right is marked *Huret*. The body is dated 1867.

The torso, arms and legs are hollow and rigid. The body is described as "blown-leather" type. It is the thickness of heavy brown leather covered with a coat of surface paint.

We believe these bodies were made under pressure in a metal mold. Leather was steamed until it was very pliable. There is only one seam down the back of the legs. The torso is made so well that no seam is apparent.

The knee and elbow joints have a type of pin that allows them to move very easily. The shoulder has two types of joints—one to allow up-and-down movement and the other to allow circular movement. The entire hip moves. This is a very rare doll with an extremely rare body.

Blown-leather bodies were satisfactory and long-lasting, but they were difficult and expensive to produce. Only a very few were made.

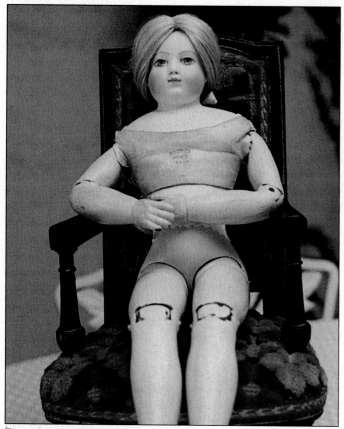

Fine blown-leather body marked *Huret*. Gutta-percha bodies for Huret dolls apparently were made in same molds. Only close examination reveals differences. Lenore Thomas doll.

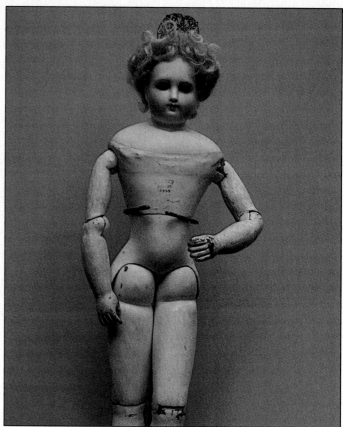

Ladylike figure of blown-leather-bodied doll. This rare doll is also marked *Huret*. Gladyse Hillsdorf doll.

LEATHER-BODIED DOLL NO. 1

The label on the body positively identifies this doll as one made by Rohmer.

The body is leather, with one handsewn seam from chest to crotch in front. There are three seams down the back and one down the back of the upper legs. There is a gusset in the hips.

Uncovered wood joints in upper arms are held in place with wood pegs. Besides these tongue-and-groove joints, an inner piece of wood goes from one arm joint to the other so when one arm is raised, the other arm raises. (This type of joint is called a *mortise-and-tenon* joint. See page 85.) From above the elbow to the hand, the arm is porcelain bisque. Arms and large bisque hands are "washer-woman" type. Fingers and thumb are separate.

Knee joints are wood, covered with leather. Feet and legs, from just below the knee, are glazed porcelain. On the tummy of the doll are two metal eyelet holes about 3/4 inch apart.

The bisque in the shoulderplate is not smooth. It is cut flat where the head is joined. There is a small, flat rim around the neck hole, and the neck ends in a small, flat rim. The rims ride against each other and allow the head to turn. This is called a *flanged neck.*

On top of the head, through the edge of the cork, are a washer and screw. We took the screw out to see how the head worked. A piece of wood with a hole fit through the shoulderplate. Around the piece of wood were several layers of leather. This arrangement kept the head in place and kept the porcelain parts from grating against each other.

The face of the doll is interesting but not beautiful. She has very white bisque that is as thin as an eggshell. This head was pressed in the mold. The mouth is painted one color, and there is no color in the nostrils.

Eyebrows are a dozen short strokes of gray. The painted blue eyes have a little gloss over the black pupil and a heavy black stroke at the edge of the lid.

Ears protrude only slightly, and they are unpierced.

The doll earned a first-place blue ribbon at the UFDC Convention in San Francisco in 1983. Her antique clothing includes striped stockings and shoes to match her peacock-green taffeta dress. We also believe the wig and hat she wears were hers originally.

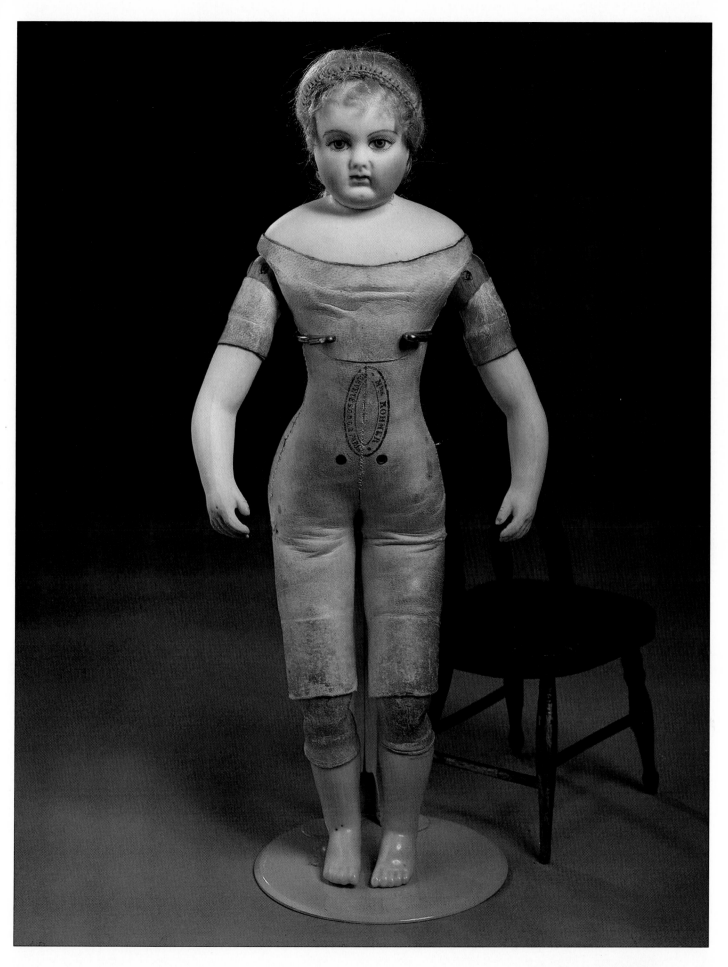

VARIATIONS

A stamped *Rohmer* body, with variations, was found by Marcia Cohen. Knees are gusseted instead of wood joints. The head has the same flanged-neck arrangement. Hips have deep gussets. The doll has glass eyes instead of painted ones.

Compare marked Rohmer bodies and heads. This one has glass eyes and gusseted knees, which shows changes made within single company. Photo courtesy Cohen Auctions.

LEATHER-BODIED DOLL NO. 2

The shoulderplate of this doll is marked *E Déposé 1 B*. Barrois is given credit for dolls marked *E Déposé B*. We consider this positive identification the doll was made by Barrois. She is 14 inches tall.

The body is handsewn leather and tightly stuffed with sawdust. It was reinforced with heavy wire that has rusted and protrudes through the leather. The front torso ends in a shield-shape, and leather cording strips cover the seam.

Arms are made of two pieces of leather with five "fingers." There is a gusset at the elbow so the arm can bend. Legs and hips are two pieces of leather with a large hip gusset and knee gusset. The feet, with *four* toes, are an additional piece. The bottom of the foot is one piece.

Hips on this doll are very well-stuffed. A cloth sack inside the torso holds sawdust.

Cheeks are well-blushed. The mouth has deeper lines around the outside, with a line between the lips. Eyes are almond-shaped and cobalt-blue. They are not paperweight eyes.

Ears are flat and pierced through the lobe into the head.

This lady doll came with drawers, petticoat, hand-knit stockings and a brown dress with black stripes. The dress was handmade and carefully lined.

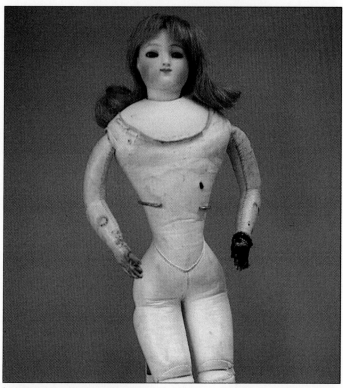

Leather-bodied dolls are common. Marked heads and shoulderplates, like marked bodies, are rare.

LEATHER-BODIED DOLLS NOs. 3 and 4

These two leather bodies were probably made by the same company. The standing doll shows improvements. Both dolls have stuffed-leather bodies. The one sitting is more crudely made and possibly older. She is marked *E 3 Déposé B* for Barrois, a very early doll maker. There are no knee joints, but hip gussets allow the doll to sit, which is unusual. Arms and glovelike hands are made of brown leather. There are no toes.

The second doll has a Huret head, and the body is stamped *Simonne*. The *Simonne* stamp was probably stamp of shop that distributed dolls. Leather fingers are unwired. She has only four toes.

Both bodies are handsewn. Note padding in chest; we checked it and found wads of wool. Both dolls are shoulder heads and good examples of leather-bodied dolls.

LEATHER-BODIED DOLL NO. 5

This is a well-made leather body by Bru. She has a Smiler head and bisque hands. The seams, shape and structure match Bru Breveté bodies. The leather that holds the shoulderplate is part of the body leather instead of an extra piece. Arms have no gussets, but joints are movable because a piece of heavy wire goes down to the bisque hand. Wire protrudes from her right arm. Note shaping of bisque hands.

LEATHER-BODIED DOLL NO. 6

A very rare old French fashion doll stands alone on a wood base. Two metal pegs, mounted on the wood stand, fit into holes in her bisque heels. Her white-kid torso is firm and stiff. She has a tiny waist and fully rounded hips. A narrow strap of kid goes over the shoulders to hold the shoulderplate on.

The doll's arms are bisque to just above the elbow, and legs are bisque to just above the knees. The legs are realistically modeled so you can see the muscles. Hands and arms are gracefully posed. Her shoulderplate has a high, modeled bust.

This doll is owned by Lenore Thomas and originally had a label on the base.

Hands, legs, feet, head and shoulderplate are realistically sculptured.

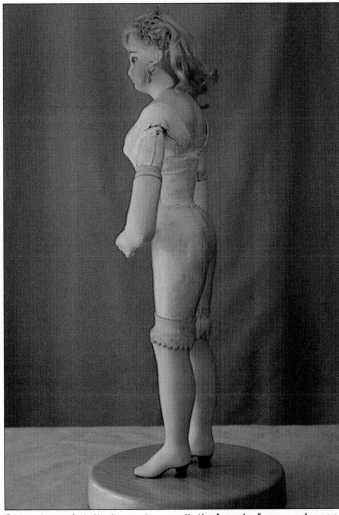

Side view of doll shows her realistic female form and pegs she stands on.

GUTTA-PERCHA-BODIED DOLL

During the 1850s, *gutta-percha* was used for heads and bodies of dolls. Gutta-percha is a gray-to-brown plastic substance, made of gutta hydrocarbon mixed with resin. Gutta is the coagulated latex of various Malaysian trees. The word gutta actually means *sap*, and the word percha means *tree*.

Gutta-percha was softened with hot water at 100F (40C) and molded at 190F (90C). It was pressed into molds and retained its shape when cooled. It was not sticky and was usually unaffected by atmosphere, but it did become brittle with age.

Some of Calixte Huret's porcelain-headed dolls, with painted eyes or glass eyes, had gutta-percha bodies. A few have survived. These bodies have wide-tongued joints in knees, hips and shoulders. Hands were also made of gutta-percha.

These bodies were made by Huret from the 1850s to the 1860s and are an important part of doll history today. The same molds were used for gutta-percha bodies as blown-leather bodies, and the same method was used to join pieces together.

When seen together in a photograph, it's impossible to tell a gutta-percha body from a blown-leather body. Both have the same painted joints, and today each body shows dark color in the joints. But upon close inspection, there is no doubt about which is which. The exposed leather is quite different from the hard, smooth surface of gutta-percha.

Gutta-percha-bodied doll marked *Huret*. Note unusual long character face of rare doll. Joints in hips are similar to those found on blown-leather bodies. Gladyse Hillsdorf doll.

Gutta-percha doll belongs to Marshall Martin. Gutta-percha became brittle with age, and few dolls with this type of body have survived.

METAL-BODIED DOLL

In our search, we found only one metal-bodied fashion doll. It has a head marked *Huret*, glass eyes and an unusual character face. She is from Gladyse Hillsdorf's collection.

Metal-bodied doll marked *Huret*. Mold for hands was same mold as used for blown-leather or gutta-percha bodies.

Recognizing Parts of French Fashion Dolls

Recognizing the different materials used for hands and feet and being able to differentiate between materials used for body parts are part of the total study of French fashion dolls. This knowledge may help you become a connoisseur of these dolls. Certain types of hands, such as bisque and wood, raise the price of a doll. Hands and feet are important clues to a doll's value and identity.

MAKERS OF FRENCH FASHION DOLLS

Our list of French fashion doll makers is only a partial one. There is much that is unknown about the dolls and the companies that made them. In the following list, we have included the most important doll makers of the fashion-doll era.

Rohmer—Marie Rohmer made dolls from 1857 to 1880. Her doll heads and bodies usually were stamped with ink in an oval on the chest. Some heads were incised *Rohmer*. Rohmer kid bodies were articulated. She made glass-eyed and painted-eyed dolls and used flanged necks and swivel necks, in addition to shoulder heads.

Some kid bodies have eyelet holes in the front. When laced, these holes make the doll sit. Rohmer dolls also had interesting knee joints. Kid feet had no indication of toes.

Metayer—We believe Metayer only distributed dolls with leather bodies. The dolls he distributed did not have leg joints or elbow joints, but arms moved at the shoulder. Dolls marked *MET* on the shoulder and *Breveté-Déposé* on the chest are probably his.

Gaultier—François Gaultier's doll heads, often marked *F.G.*, with swivel necks and bisque shoulderplates are found on gusseted kid bodies. (For an explanation and clarification of the Gaultier name and spelling, see our book *How to Collect French Bébé Dolls*, also published by HPBooks.) Some bodies have jointed wood arms and hands. The F.G. head is also found on all-wood bodies that are articulated at the knee, hip, elbow and shoulder, with an added twist joint in upper legs and upper arms. F.G. heads also have been found on cloth bodies. Nearly all these

---

Left: 25-inch Portrait Jumeau with "collar" shoulderplate and swivel head. Shoulderplate is unusually large and deep, giving her a bosom. Tinted-bisque hands are expressive and well-formed. Body is leather with gusseted joints. Dress and decoration are muted maroon brocade, except for lace inset in front. Rows of puckered, ruffled material are used at sleeves and across back shoulder. Dress has soft pleats and appears to be original to doll. Small Mascotte child doll rides stuffed horse and little R.D. (Rabery and Delphieu) child doll tugs at her skirt. Large doll is also shown on page 21.

Marked Rohmer doll with expression-less flat eyes and fine white bisque. Wig is human hair and probably a replacement.

Portrait doll has gentle lip shaping and soft painting. Hand-knotted mohair wig is braided and knotted in back.

Doll is marked *E.B.* Note lower shoulderplate. Barrois made dolls beginning in late 1860s.

dolls with F.G. heads had glass eyes and pierced ears. See exception on page 124. Recently we found a rare F.G.-marked doll with painted eyes and a shoulder head.

Some heads by Gaultier were marked *F.G.* in a cartouche (scroll). The size and shape of the cartouche varies, as if drawn by hand. Others heads were marked *F.C.G.* but not in a scroll.

F.G. heads are also found on Gesland bodies, which are stockinette bodies with metal armatures. These are similar to the child Gesland body, except the doll had a mature ladylike figure.

Jumeau—The Jumeau Co. was started by Pierre François Jumeau; he was later joined by his son Emile. The company made porcelain-headed dolls with articulated bodies. Some were wood-bodied dolls with porcelain heads, and some were kid-bodied lady dolls.

A few Jumeau heads found on fashion dolls are marked with typical Jumeau marks, and others have only check marks. Some bodies were stamped *Jumeau*. We found one Jumeau-marked body with a bisque head, a shoulderplate with a molded bosom and graceful bisque hands.

Jumeau fashion dolls seem to have numbers for sizes. The smaller numbers are for smaller

dolls. Numbers are incised on the heads. For more on the sizes of bodies, see page 115.

E.B.—The initials E.B. are for E. Barrois. Many fashion dolls are found with the mark *E Déposé B* incised on the front of the shoulderplate. It is found on dolls with shoulder heads, swivel heads and flanged necks. There seem to be many kinds of bodies with the E.B.-marked head, including an all-leather body, a leather body with bisque hands to just above the wrist and a stuffed body somewhat similar to a cloth-covered Gesland body. The cloth-covered body had bisque hands and feet.

One very strange E.B.-marked lady doll we have seen has two rows of teeth, an open mouth and glass eyes. The doll is a shoulder head.

Terrene—Another strange fashion body is marked *Terrene*. The bisque swivel head is on a shoulderplate. The body is leather, and upper arms and knees are metal. The doll has wood legs and bisque arms with the elbow joint cast in the bisque. Hips are unjointed, but leather was left unstuffed so legs could be moved easily. Terrene was listed as a doll maker in Paris from 1863 to 1890.

Verry Fils (Sons)—Most kid bodies made by this company were stamped *Verry Fils*. Records

Right: 13-inch, unmarked swivel-head doll has cobalt-blue eyes. Wig is mohair, and ears are pierced into head. Crude, hand-sewn leather body spills sawdust. Hands are mittenlike, with fingers indicated by stitching. No toes are indicated. Handsewn skirt and fitted jacket of dark teal-blue silk are lined with tan fabric. Skirt has modified train with extra bustle. Fine black-silk lace is used as trim around skirt, jacket and bustle. Silver buttons close jacket front. Old leather side-button boots have same buttons. Boots also have tassels in front. Turquoise velvet hat is trimmed with teal feathers and black lace.

Left: Marked *T*, doll has swivel head, long lambswool wig and blue paperweight eyes.

do not indicate whether the company made dolls or distributed them. Verry dolls have bisque swivel necks, shoulderplates and glass eyes. Bodies are kid with gusseted joints. There are no marks on the heads.

Simonne—Today, many French fashion dolls are found with *Simonne* stamped in blue on the chest. We believe Simonne was a distributor or assembler of dolls rather than a doll-making company making porcelain heads.

Head types of dolls marked *Simonne* include the flanged neck, shoulder head and swivel head. Bodies are kid or leather, with bisque arms or kid arms and kid legs.

Schmitt and Fils (Sons)—The firm of Schmitt and Fils started in the doll and toy business in 1863. They probably made complete lady dolls, but we have only hearsay evidence from European doll collectors that a marked Schmitt fashion doll exists.

Bru—The Bru establishment, founded by Casimir Bru, was listed in the Paris doll-maker directory as early as 1868. The Bru Co. made and dressed many lady dolls. They made a wood body that was articulated with a ball-joint at the waist. We also have found leather and kid bodies with Bru heads. Some bodies had bisque hands and wood feet; other heads were found on bodies that were the all-leather type.

After studying dolls found in boxes and reading an antique Bru catalog, we learned Bru used letters for sizes on fashion dolls. The closer the letter is to the letter A, the smaller the doll. Some Bru shoulderplates are marked B. *Jne et Cie.* and *Déposé* on the shoulder. Sometimes Bru heads have *Déposé* incised on the front top of the head, under the hair, and a letter on the back. Bru made shoulder heads and swivel heads.

Huret—The name Calixte Huret was associated with doll making beginning in 1850. She appears to have been a genius in the doll world—she is credited with many inventions and made improvements in wood bodies and joints. Successors in her company apparently did not make French fashion dolls.

In 1850, she applied for a patent for an articulated, molded doll body. In 1855, she was using gutta-percha for jointed lady bodies. These bodies are extremely rare today, but one was exhibited at the UFDC Convention in San Antonio, Texas, in 1984. It was brittle, but joints were movable. The rare doll was owned and exhibited by Marshall Martin, a specialist in Huret dolls.

Huret dolls are found with a stamp on the

Right: 17-inch Smiler marked *D*. She has swivel head, gray paperweight eyes and pierced ears. Wig is undyed human hair in elaborate, net-covered coiffure. She wears one original emerald-green earring. Arms were replaced. Her exquisite handmade underclothing is antique. Green silk costume is replacement and was copied from original. Stitching and decorations match. Note trim on skirt bottom—it was commonly used by couturiers. Doubled-fabric strip is gathered, turned and fastened at intervals over ruffle at bottom. Around her neck she wears binoculars. Umbrella is silk-and-lace on ivory handle. Green shoes are high-heeled, shaped slippers with flat bow and gold buckles on toes. Doll is also shown on page 123.

chest of leather bodies or gutta-percha bodies. Slender, wood-articulated bodies with metal hands are unmarked, as are an assortment of other bodies.

Shoulder heads on Huret dolls have short, fat necks. Swivel heads have a similar face but longer necks. Some Huret dolls have necks that have a roll or ridge of bisque next to the shoulderplate. A few Huret dolls have heart-shaped shoulderplates. See page 90. Some Huret heads have elongated faces with glass eyes.

Huret was probably the inventor of the swivel head, even though others claimed the invention as theirs. Her early swivel heads had a tube of porcelain extending beyond the rounded neck that ended in the shoulderplate.

These wonderful creations can still be found in original cotton costumes decorated with soutache-braid designs.

Steiner—Jules Nicholas Steiner was in the doll-making business as early as 1855, but little is known about his lady dolls. His early dolls were unmarked. We know he made some very early dolls with open mouths and teeth and some walking lady dolls.

We have no way to establish definitely which companies made heads, bodies or costumes. We know some companies were assemblers of dolls or that they put dolls together from parts made elsewhere.

Unmarked Dolls—There are many marked and unmarked dolls that we will never be able to attribute to any maker. So be it. We don't have the names of the people who created the fabulous costumes either. The dolls and costumes are works of art. Study and learn about each doll, but collect and love dolls for their beauty and historic value.

EXPLANATION OF JOINTS

It's important as a collector of French fashion dolls to be aware of the different types of joints you may find. Read the following information, and see photos on pages 86 and 87. Refer to the section on bodies and material, beginning on page 44.

Tongue-and-Groove Joint—This joint has a tongue or extension of wood that fits exactly

Starry, gray-paperweight eyes almost overwhelm well-painted little head. Doll is unmarked.

into a groove of wood. The joint is not glued to allow easy back-and-forth movement.

Mortise-and-Tenon Joint—A tenon (projection of wood) is shaped to fit the mortise (hole or notch) in another piece of wood. The joint is movable or fixed in place and unmovable. When used at the shoulder, it may make both arms move at the same time.

Ball-and-Socket Joint—This is a partially carved wood ball placed in a socket, which allows limited movement in any direction. This type of joint is used in knees, elbows, wrists, hips and shoulders.

Wood Pegs—Tiny, hand-whittled straight pegs

Left: Rare, early doll marked *Huret* is very pale bisque. Ears are flat and unpierced, and eyes are painted blue. There is some glaze over eyes to give them wet look. Lid has black line, and eyelashes are black. Eyebrows are soft and light brown. Wig is blond mohair. She wears old bonnet of thin, stiff cotton. These bonnets were sometimes worn under heavier bonnet or hooded cape. This type of bonnet is found on dolls from 1855 to 1865 and often is worn with midcalf cotton dresses decorated with soutache braid. Doll is also shown on page 14.

Joints used in fashion dolls were not entirely new. They were used in these old peg wood dolls.

Early mannequins show same intricate joints. This one has joints in ankles, wrists and waist, as well as hips, shoulders and knees.

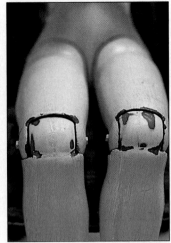
Pin joints were rarely used on leather. Metal pin goes through two knee sections. Effect is similar to tongue-and-groove joint.

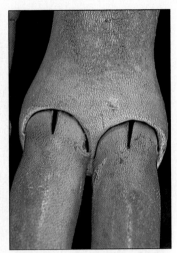
Variation of tongue-and-groove joint. This Jumeau body has metal disk instead of wood tongue to allow full hip movement.

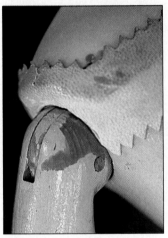
Tongue-and-groove shoulder joint fastened with wood peg. Tongue that extends into arm is round or disk-shaped.

Arm of Phenix body shows how tongue-and-groove elbow joint moves on wood pin that goes through arm.

Tongue-and-groove joint is used with ball-joint for wrist movement.

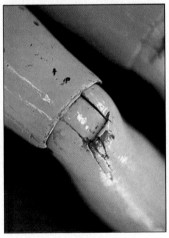
Knee joint ends in ball and has tongue-and-groove for movement.

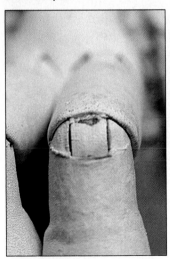
Neatly covered tongue-and-groove knee joint.

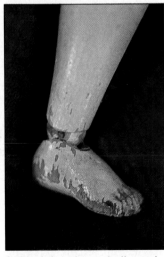
Ankle joint shows ball used for movement.

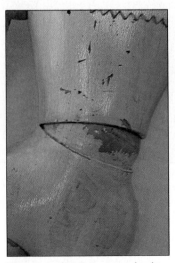
Rare ball-joint used in waist allows doll to be posed in natural positions.

Twist joints, found in waist, upper leg and upper arm, can be turned for more-natural positioning.

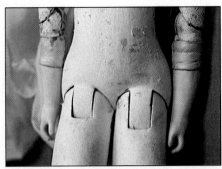

Tongue-and-groove hip joint covered with leather.

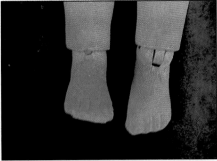

Tongue-and-groove joint used in ankles with ball-joint in silk twill-covered body.

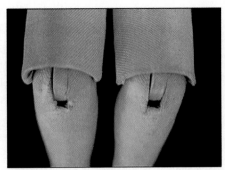

Tongue part of knee joint is 3/8-inch-thick piece of semicircular wood attached to upper leg.

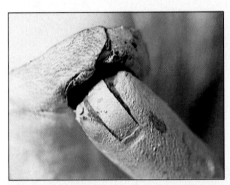

Mortise-and-tenon joint used in shoulder. Dowel (tenon) goes through shoulder section, into hole (mortise) in each arm joint to allow both arms to raise or lower at same time.

Combination ball-and-socket joint with tongue-and-groove joint in shoulder. Small round spots are ends of wood pins that hold parts together.

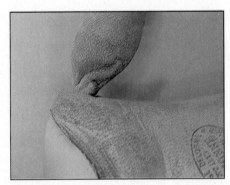

Unstuffed joints, without sawdust or hair stuffing, were used in leather bodies. Joints allowed arms and legs to swing loosely.

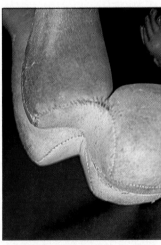

Gussets in leather bodies are most-common, poorest-working joints used on French fashions. Gussets are oval patches of leather, set in hips, knees and elbows of leather bodies to allow limited movement.

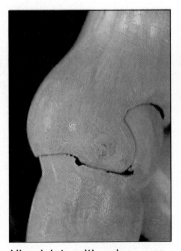

Hip joint with pins was unique combination of shapes that fit together. It was held by one metal pin going entire width of body.

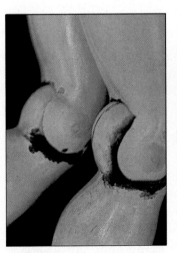

Underside of knee joints shows they were two pieces. Blob on side is metal-pin fastening.

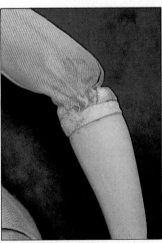

Gesland stockinette-covered, metal-armature joints are different. They move only in back-and-forth direction with rivet holding two pieces of metal.

used to fasten parts of wood bodies together.

Combination Ball-and-Socket, Tongue-and-Groove Joint—This type of joint is used in hips and shoulders of some wood dolls to give circular *and* up-and-down movement.

Twist Joint—This is a joint used in upper legs, upper arms and sometimes in the waist. It allows movement backward and forward, in one direction only. Legs or arms can be twisted into lifelike poses, such as sitting with legs crossed. The joint was used on Gesland wood bodies with F.G. heads.

Gussets—Oval patches of extra material were added to leather bodies to facilitate movement.

Unstuffed Joint—In a stuffed body, an area is left unstuffed that allows the joint to move. Sometimes arms or legs were stitched above or below to keep stuffing from getting into the joint.

Pin Joint—A metal pin holds an arm or leg into the upper arm or leg section and allows it to move. This type of joint was also used in some hips and shoulders.

Gesland Joint—Metal armature of flat metal strips is put together with rivetlike joints so it moves in one direction. The body is padded and covered with knit fabric over the armature.

Disk Joint—A covered, washerlike disk of metal or wood in a shoulder moves against a covered disk in the upper arm. This type of joint was rarely used in hips.

Wire Joint—This is not really a joint. Wire inside stuffed-leather arms and fingers allows them to be moved or posed in different positions.

HANDS

Hands were made of many materials, and they were made in many shapes and sizes. Some hands were in proportion to the doll, and some were not.

The most common hand is leather with wired fingers; they are probably hands of later dolls. The rarest hand may be the hand of solid wood, either jointed or unjointed at the wrist.

Many different types and colors of leather were used for hands. Some hands were formed into mitten shapes, and others had five fingers. There are many delicate, lovely bisque hands. We have even found cloth, gutta-percha, metal and blown- or pressed-leather hands.

HEADS

The two most common types of head and shoulder arrangements for French fashion dolls

Shoulder-head doll is 17 inches tall. Kid-over-jointed-wood body has bisque arms and swivel waist. Costume of silk-taffeta and lace is from her trousseau. She has many outfits, including nightgowns, coats, evening capes, corset, muffs and hats. Doll, from Cohen Auctions, sold in 1984 for $2500.

are the *swivel head* and *shoulder head*. Doll makers also used other types and variations of head and shoulder arrangements. Below we discuss the different types we have found.

Swivel Head—The head and shoulderplate are two separate pieces held together with a spring arrangement. See page 126 for explanation of spring arrangement. The spring arrangement allows the head to turn and bend forward and backward. A doll with a swivel head can be posed more easily than other types of heads. See page 90.

Shoulder Head—The head and shoulderplate are *one* piece. The head cannot move or turn. Dealers refer to these dolls as *stiff necks*. See page 90.

Flanged Neck—The neck goes straight down and fits against a flattened area on a separate shoulderplate. The head turns but does not tip backward or forward. See page 90.

Wood hands from Jumeau body. Surface paint is flaking off.

Mitten-type leather hand.

Early brown-leather hand with separate fingers.

Gutta-percha hand on Huret doll.

Metal hand on Phenix body.

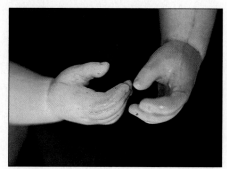

Repaired bisque hands of Rohmer doll.

Bisque hand found on Gesland stockinette-covered bodies.

Bisque hand of Rohmer wood body covered with leather.

Graceful bisque hands of leather-bodied Bru doll.

Shoulderplate—A shoulderplate is a separate plate of bisque that covers a doll's shoulders. The bisque was used to make a pleasant-appearing shoulder and to secure a swivel head to the body.

Collar Shoulderplate—This is used with a regular swivel head, but the shoulderplate turns up and forms a collarlike arrangement around the neck, instead of being flat around the indentation for the swivel. For a clarification of this, see photo on page 90. This type of neck-and-head arrangement is found on Portrait Jumeaus. You may find the same arrangement on other dolls.

Heart Shoulderplate—A heart-shaped or point is shaped into the hollow of the shoulderplate on some Huret dolls. This arrangement makes the neck look longer. See photo on next page.

Decorated Shoulderplates—Occasionally we find a fashion doll with jewels or even miniature scenes incorporated into the decoration of the shoulderplate. Gladyse Hillsdorf has several of these in her collection. See photo on following page. One also can be seen in the Margaret Strong Museum in Rochester, New York.

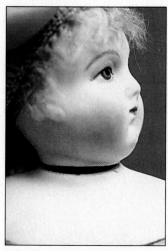

Flanged-neck arrangement on marked Rohmer doll.

Wood and leather in flanged neck hold head on. Screw goes from top of cork pate to wood piece in neck.

Shoulder head is also called *stiff neck*.

Swivel head with shoulderplate allows head to turn and bend forward or backward.

Collar shoulderplate is early version of shoulderplate that had roll of porcelain around neck hole.

Valentine or *sweetheart* neck used by Huret. Shoulderplate is cut to point in center.

THE SMILER

The face with "the Mona Lisa smile," called the *Smiler,* is often found on French fashion dolls. For many years, collectors and dealers have argued over its origin. Some say the head is by Bru, while others say it was made by Jumeau. Some say it is neither. Many questions from this period may never be answered. Dolls were toys or fashion models; they were not made as signed pieces of art to leave as legacies.

We have spent a lot of time studying Smilers. It appears to us that there are *three* different faces, and they are only slightly different. The differences could be a variation of an original mold. Or one doll maker could have copied another's mold and changed it slightly. A third explanation could be slight changes were made

Gladyse Hillsdorf doll has coveted jeweled shoulderplate showing church in Paris. 16-inch doll is dressed in original clothes. She was made by E. Rocharde and is marked *Déposé.*

Sought-after Smilers cost more money than many other fashion dolls. This Smiler is dressed in original gray, blue and white printed silk. Blue at sleeves and hat brings out her blue eyes. Lenore Thomas doll.

Almond-eyed Smiler has blue eyes, arched brows and pierced ears. Lenore Thomas doll.

in the cleanup of greenware. It's easy to make eyes larger or rounder or change the indentation between lips in the greenware stage. It is possible the decorator slightly changed the painting of the mouth. All painting was done freehand so it's bound to vary slightly.

We must also consider another fact in deciding who made these heads. In the 1860s and '70s, most doll makers did not have kilns to fire heads. They did not have equipment to prepare the clay nor did they have designers or mold makers. Making doll heads was a very complicated procedure.

For these reasons, some doll makers had a porcelain company or china factory make and mark heads for them. Sometimes heads were purchased in the whiteware stage—fired bisque but unpainted—and the doll maker did the painting. China painting requires only a low firing temperature, and this could be managed with less equipment.

The Smilers we have found have letters and numbers for sizes but no other markings. Heads have been found on articulated wood bodies, with or without a waist joint. They have been found on all-kid bodies resembling the Bru Breveté body and combination bodies of wood and kid.

An old book, *The Jumeau Doll Story* (written in 1885 and translated by Nina Davies), describes doll production by Jumeau. It contains a photo of a Poupée Parisienne, Jumeau's name for a French fashion doll. The doll has a Smiler head. Some would say this is positive proof Jumeau made Smiler dolls.

In the Colemans' book, *The Collector's Book of Doll Clothes*, published in 1975 by Crown Publishers, they call attention to Bru doll boxes of 1872 that show wood-armed dolls with Smiler heads. Casimir Bru obtained a patent for these bodies with wood arm joints, but he may not have actually made the heads.

Smiler has narrow eyes and wood body. She is marked 2. Doll is dressed in tissue silk-organza with blue stripes. Dress has full skirt and bustle and is trimmed with hand-knotted fringe.

Some people believe this proves Bru made the Smiler. We draw no definite conclusions as to who made Smilers or which companies used them. With more research, we believe someone may discover one firm produced these heads for several companies.

STUDYING THE HEAD

Bisque—Study the bisque head of a fashion doll. Look inside it—it should be pure white. All fashion dolls were made of white porcelain, which is very thin and translucent.

We sometimes hear people say they like "pale bisque" or "dark bisque." Actually, the color is not the color of the bisque but color that was applied to the *outside* of the head. Bisque heads were usually dipped once or twice in flesh-colored paint. The more the head was dipped,

the darker the color. Later dolls were more highly colored, and a few early dolls were not dipped in flesh-colored paint but were left white.

Painting—Study the painting of the doll head. Sometimes as many as three colors were used on an old doll for lips, and two colors were used in the nostrils. When you study painting on a fashion doll, note where cheek blush was placed. Sometimes you can match up dolls and doll makers by studying and comparing painting.

Eyebrows painted by one company usually look similar in color and strokes because companies established painting techniques. The shape of lips is usually also similar in each company.

Ears—Ears are interesting on lady dolls. Some ears were *applied*, which means ears were stuck on a head in the greenware stage. Other ears were flattened out and made in the mold. Some ears seem to be out of place, such as Huret ears, which are placed too far back on the head.

Ears were pierced two ways. Those on tiny, early heads had a hole pierced through the lobe *into* the head. This made it difficult to repair earrings because the wig and pate had to be taken off to find the wire that fastened the earring. The wire loop on the outside of the ear was supposed to be permanent, so different earrings could be attached more easily from outside the head, but they weren't.

Later, ears were pierced through the ear lobe, which was more convenient.

Eyes—Eyes of French fashion dolls were painted on the face, or they were glass eyes that were set into the head. Dolls with painted eyes and glass eyes were sold at the same time. Glass-eyed dolls were more expensive.

Glass eyes could be the older, flat type (usually cobalt-blue) or paperweight eyes. Old paperweight eyes are exceptionally beautiful. They are found in gray, several shades of blue, amber, brown and even tricolor. See page 107 for a photo of tricolored eyes.

Often a dark line around the pupil was used to enhance eye color. Glass and paperweight eyes were set. They were put in the doll's head with wax, then plaster was put over the back of the eyes to hold them in place. Glass and paperweight eyes were handmade, and often they did not match.

Right: Smiler is also shown on page 4. Almond-shaped paperweight eyes are very narrow. Darker, outer rim of iris was drawn into lighter color to give rayed effect. Eyebrows are five lines, and eyelashes are fine pewter gray. Ears are pierced through lobe, and head was pressed. Doll's blond-mohair wig is sparse, hand-knotted mohair. Compare shape of this doll's face with other Smilers.

Above: Small swivel-headed doll with hand-knotted, human-hair wig and flat blue eyes.

Left: Swivel-headed doll has droopy cheeks and large, pale-blue paperweight eyes.

Eye holes for glass eyes were handcut without a template, and holes were not always perfect. Remember this when looking at old dolls, and the mismatched eye holes won't bother you as much. Usually the space around glass eyes was filled with wax. If the doll had been stored in a hot attic, wax may have melted and left a space.

Faces—The faces of fashion dolls portrayed different types of people. Some faces are pleasant looking. Some are character faces, and others are portrait types. Some lady dolls have long faces with smiling mouths. Others have plump cheeks and prissy little mouths.

When you begin studying fashion dolls, the variations in faces will intrigue you. You may even be tempted to name them. Be careful you don't name them for people you know.

EARS

We have found four types of ears on French fashion dolls. The ears help us date a doll. The earliest dolls had very poorly defined ears, which were very close to the head, and they were unpierced. The mold usually left a vertical mark across the ear. Often, from the front, it appears the doll has no ears. See photos on next page.

Then doll makers began piercing ears. Ears were still flat, crude and close to the head, but the ear lobe was pierced through to the *inside* of the bisque head. Two ends of a wire were pushed through the hole, then bent over inside the head. This left a tiny loop on the *outside* of the head. As long as the loop was there, earrings could be changed by attaching them to the outside loop. Often the loop was taken out or it fell out, then the wig and pate had to be removed to change the earrings.

French fashion dolls larger than 20 inches had applied ears. These ears were made in a separate mold and attached to the head in the greenware stage. Ears were pierced through the lobe. Fine wire was put in the lobe as a convenience.

Ears were better modeled as time passed, and the ear lobe was pulled away from the head a little, even though ears were made in the mold. These ears were also pierced through the lobe, and earrings were easily attached.

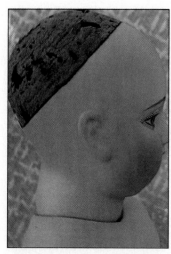

Unpierced ear of very old French fashion doll.

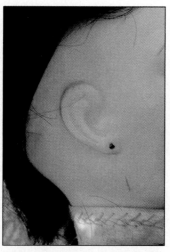

Ear with pierced-into-the-head lobe.

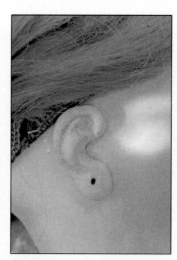

Applied ear, which was pierced, of Portrait fashion Jumeau.

Ear pierced only through lobe. Ear was made in head mold.

BODY LABELS AND STAMPS OF FRENCH FASHION DOLLS

Some French fashion dolls have labels stamped in ink on leather bodies. Sometimes a label indicates the shop that dressed and sold the doll. Occasionally a label is the mark of an establishment that bought heads, made bodies and assembled dolls. On Huret dolls, the body label indicates the entire doll was made by Huret. Discovering facts such as these makes studying lady fashion dolls intriguing.

The stamps, marks and labels shown here and on the next page were copied from worn bodies. Many are nearly illegible, and some are incomplete or misread because of a label's faintness. Use the following information to compare labels on French fashion dolls you may have.

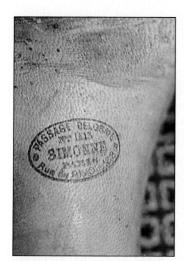

Oval blue *Simonne* stamp is probably stamp of shop selling dolls.

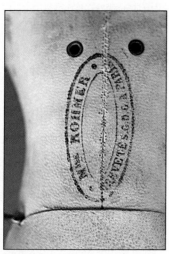

Rohmer in blue oval is sometimes placed across body.

Extremely rare brass plate marked *Phenix.* Lenore Thomas doll.

There are several variations of this blue *Huret* stamp.

Body Stamps—The following are body stamps we have found on various dolls:

J. TERRENE
10 Rue du Marché S. Honové
PARIS

Aux GALLERIESDEFER
    VERRY FILS
1989 Des ITALIENS

PASSAGE DEL ORME
    No. la 10
    SIMONNE
    Paris

Rue DE RIVOLI 188
ROHMER
BREVETÉ SGDG PARIS

A. METAYER
22 RUE S. Martin Tours

Aux REVES de L'ENFRANCE
SPECIALITÉ de POUPÉES
40 R. De RICHELIEU PARIS

HURET
22 Bouleo d Mont Matre
Paris

JUMEAU
Medaille D'OR
PARIS

● One doll we saw with the head marked *F.G.* has the label, shown below, attached to her leather body. Many F.G. heads are found on Gesland-stamped bodies.

Au POUPÉ MAGASIN
    des Enfantes
Passage de L'opera
    Paris

● The label shown in the next column is stamped in green ink and was found on a pressed-leather body. It could be a label for Victor Pierre Clement, who obtained a patent for pressed-leather bodies around 1870. Pressed-leather bodies may be the same as blown-leather bodies. Our doll is stamped *Huret*.

Vve CLEMENT
Solidité Garantie

● The label shown below is stamped in blue and occasionally found on very old leather bodies between 12 and 14 inches tall. Heads are unmarked.

Aux ENFANTES Sares
    GUITON
Passage
PARIS

● The label below is stamped in a brass oval label found on the wood body of a rare fashion doll owned by Lenore Thomas. The body is similar to the scarce Martin body, except it does not have ankle joints.

Bte SGDG
LA POUPÉE
PHENIX
MARQUE DÉPOSÉ

● Mme. Lavelee Peronne produced, or was connected with, one or more periodicals that dealt with doll and child fashions. She had a main shop in Paris, with as many as 200 people working for her, and her shop produced the finest French fashions and complete trousseaus for dolls. Her label was:

A La POUPÉE DE NUREMBERG
21 Rue de Choiseul
Paris

● One leather body we found was labeled *Mme. Peronne*, but we have found no evidence she produced the doll body—yet she may have. It is more probable that Peronne, like Simonne, costumed dolls, then put on her address stamp or name on the doll's body.

● The label shown below is stamped in blue on a blown-leather body.

MEDAILLE D'ARGENT
    Huret
22 Bouleut d'Montmartre, Paris
    EXP. Univer NLE 1869

● Heads signed *Ed. Rocharde, Breveté SGDG* have a half-sphere set into the shoulderplate with scenes of Paris or religious scenes. See page 90.

● The oval green-blue stamp shown in the next column is found on some shoulder heads with almond-shaped glass eyes. This is probably the label of a doll shop.

Au Parades Des Enfantes
Mon REMOND
156 Rue Rivoli VOL 155

● In December 1984, Marcia Cohen of Cohen Auctions, displayed a wood-bodied fashion doll in her auction catalog. The doll had joints in the ankles, knees, hips, waist, shoulders, elbows and hands. The body still had part of the original paper label on the back of the torso. It was marked *A. Gesl——*. The remaining letters were missing, but we believe it is a Gesland body. It is the first time we have found *any* kind of label on a wood body of this type.

WIGS

Wigs were usually made of wool, mohair or human hair. To establish a dating sequence, fur, lambswool or unborn lambskin and various other animal skins with soft hair were used first. Fur was usually trimmed to about 1 inch, then matted down. It was sometimes dyed. Lambswool was left curly, or it was straightened. Unborn lambskin made an interesting wig of tiny, tight curls. We have found unborn-lambskin wigs in yellow tones and gray.

As wig-making was refined, the next material used was soft, versatile mohair or Tibetan-goat hair. This came in many colors, such as brown and blond, and many shades in between. It took dyes very well. Many hairstyles could be created on mohair wigs. Long, tiny curls could be made, and hair could be easily braided. With mohair, fancy hairstyles could be created on a small scale.

Later, French fashion dolls had human-hair wigs. Human hair was coarse and not as becoming as mohair wigs on fashion dolls, but mohair was difficult to obtain.

Today, many antique fashion dolls wear replacement wigs of human hair. Many replacement wigs come from France. There is also a wool-fiber wig made for lady dolls, but wool-fiber wigs all seem to look alike.

Originally wigs on French fashion dolls were attached to the cork pate with small nails. Many nailed-on wigs are still found on dolls. Most nails have been replaced with glue.

STYLES OF WIGS

Below is a list of hairstyles used on fashion dolls. They are listed in sequence from the 1850s to the 1890s. See photos of some different styles below.
1. Hair drawn back with little curls over ears.
2. Hair drawn to top of head with curls on each side of face.
3. Hair center-parted with bun; ears showing.
4. Hair center-parted with short curls; back hair braided and tied to head.
5. Braids wrapped around head or across top of head.
6. Bun at back of neck covered with net.
7. Large bun low on back of head.
8. Hair drawn back with braid wrapped around head and many curls down back.
9. Hair center-parted with two braids down

Gold-mohair wig shown on Jumeau doll has tiny braids, bun in back and four large curls in front.

Original style of mohair wig has antique ribbon and fine curls down back of doll's neck.

Hair on this Jumeau is pulled up on one side, and three long curls hang over her left ear.

Neatly braided, old mohair wig with string curls in front of ears. Hair was covered with net.

back. (This type of hairstyle was used on dolls that wore provincial costumes.)

10. Hair center-parted with braid wrapped over top.

11. Hair center-parted with curls on both sides.

12. Orange blossoms worked into hair, such as for a bride.

13. Hair long and loose.

14. Hair combed flat in front; high curls in back, decorated with flowers.

15. Ribbons across front.

16. Bangs or short curls in front, with hair styled in various ways in back.

In studying many French fashion dolls, it appears owners played with the hair. Some changed wigs or even the type of wig. It is very difficult to determine if a wig is a doll's original.

We have included a quote for fun but also to tell you how white or violet hair was given a "powdered look" when dressing French fashion dolls in ball gowns. This quote from *Lady's Friend*, a magazine published in 1865, describes the procedure. "The best manner of powdering the hair for a fancy ball is to rub the surface well with lard, then use plain violet powder freely. After washing the hair the following morning, all traces of powder and lard will disappear. The lard causes the powder to cling to the hair, and neither of the ingredients is injurious."

French fashion doll with trunk and gowns for sale at UFDC doll convention.

LADY'S TRUNK AND TROUSSEAU

It's a joy to find a lady doll complete with her trunk. It is a treasure if you find a trunk that still has many original items. It's fun to discover the different types of trunks—little trunks, big trunks, trunks that were papered inside, trunks with trays on the inside and straps and handles on the outside. And it's fun to go through the beautiful accessories inside.

Listed below are items we have seen or found in various Parisian doll trunks:

red-flannel petticoat	boots
apron	earrings
toothbrush	Bible
embroidered white petticoat	shoes
	hat box
scarf	cup and saucer
scissors	nightdress
chemise	hats
fur collar and muff	travel rug
soap in dish	bedjacket
plain underdrawers	purse with chain handle
gloves—2 sets	
mirror	fringed shawl
underdrawers with tucks and lace	coat and hat
	day dress
jewelry	pincushion
perfume bottle	parasols
white stockings	ball gown
watches	fans
corsets	ribbons
fancy stockings	comb
pearls	powder-puff box
hairpins	shoe horn

From what we have discovered, Huret, Rohmer, Bru, Jumeau, Barrois and Gaultier were the largest producers of fine lady dolls with professionally made trousseaus and trunks. The items included in the trunk influenced the price of the doll and trunk. Originally, little items could be purchased through doll shops or catalogs as gifts for a child and added to the original trunk.

Doll's trunk shows some accessories.

Fashion-Doll Collectors

There are a half-million doll collectors in the United States, and they collect many different kinds of dolls. Even in the relatively small number of fashion-doll collectors and fashion-doll collections, there is a great deal of variety. After studying different collections, we have identified some themes around which fine collections have been built or are being built. These are described below. French fashions are classics from the past to treasure for generations to come.

The types of fashion dolls that people collect may be influenced by things beyond their control. Sometimes a doll club helps you learn and inspires you to be a good collector. Some collectors live near auctions, conventions and doll shows; others are isolated and do their collecting by mail or absentee bidding. These factors affect the quality and quantity of a collection. The amount of money a collector can spend also has a lot to do with which dolls are purchased. Even the size of doll cabinets may influence what is collected.

Types of Collections—Collections of *one-of-a-kind* French fashion dolls are probably the most numerous, and they tend to be the largest. Collectors love the costumes, faces and bodies of lady dolls. Some collectors prefer only *marked French fashions*, but this keeps a collection very small.

Advanced fashion-doll collectors often look for *unusual bodies*. They find quality and craftsmanship in polished, articulated wood bodies. They find character in the century-old, smooth-working ball-joints and tongue-and-groove joints. They find excitement in rare combinations of leather, cloth, wood and bisque. They often exhibit their rare dolls unclothed so others can enjoy the beautiful bodies.

Collectors of fashion dolls with *different* and *unusual faces* have many dolls to choose from. When collecting, they consider types of eyes and ears and the painting of a doll. They look for dolls dressed to bring out special features. This type of collector wants a few bisque dolls that

---

Left: Gaultier made this marked 18-inch fashion doll. She wears original costume of soft, deep-green satin with pink pinstripe. Dress appears to have been made commercially—all seams are machine-sewn. Costume has fitted bodice and full skirt with elaborate bustle. Lace was added at neck and sleeves.

worth buying. Some collectors are interested only in original costumes. With proper care, original costumes probably will last many years; then they can be copied.

Historic Value—French fashion dolls, whether dressed or not, in good or poor condition, are of historic value. Collect them while their prices are still low—they must be preserved!

The points discussed above affect the prices of fashion dolls. They also affect the value of dolls, but considering their age, French fashion dolls are valuable and worth collecting.

Decide what is important to you. Your collection should make you happy and give you joy every time you see it. Don't consider the opinion of friends or members of your doll club. Do your own thing, and buy what you can afford. Some collectors are like us—they prefer dolls to diamonds any day.

FASHION DOLLS AS AN INVESTMENT

Many people collect certain dolls because of their special appeal. Often, without being aware of it, it is the study, education and knowledge of the background of dolls that makes us prefer or choose a particular one. It is not instinct, as a collector may say, but accumulation of knowledge or developed good taste. If you have a natural love of French dolls, you probably look for information and search for knowledge. You need to know more about French dolls, and it is a continuing, exhaustive search.

By studying French fashion dolls—by studying each part and focusing on quality—we hope to increase your awareness of these dolls.

Setting Standards for Collecting—We are concerned about the quality of the dolls being purchased and feel standards must be set. We want to share our standards with beginners so they are able to criticize, analyze and discuss standards of dolls. This will help you develop a basic understanding and appreciation of other collections. If a doll is worth caring about, share the knowledge with other collectors. Beautiful old dolls give lasting pleasure, while the newer, modern dolls (*not* reproduction bisque dolls) are not as appealing.

With French fashion dolls, as with most other dolls, certain qualities make them a good

Expression eyes are beautiful tricolored eyes. Lenore Thomas doll.

investment. Many people do not collect fashion dolls as an investment because they don't understand their value. Men collectors are more investment-oriented and want to purchase a doll that will increase in value—perhaps as much as 20% a year.

After working with dolls for many years, and making many mistakes, we feel the characteristics described below help increase a doll's value. These characteristics are:

1. Scarcity or rarity.
2. Original condition and original costume.
3. Quality.
4. Beauty.
5. Markings.

We believe *scarcity* or *rarity* may be one of the most important factors. If a type of doll is plentiful and there is one in every collection, you can't expect the doll to increase much in value.

Left: Doll with Bru leather body marked *C.* Double chin and heavy eyelids are similar to, and perhaps the same as, other Smilers. Eye holes are circled with black. Eyelashes are gray, and eyebrows are strokes of deep amber. She wears original curled, sparse red-blond mohair wig over cork pate. Head is pressed bisque with ears pierced through lobe. Upper ear is flat, but lobe was brought forward for easier piercing. Hat is woven straw and decorated with black velvet and gold ornament.

Crude bisque, cloth-bodied doll with painted blue eyes is dressed as fisherwoman carrying net and shells. Costume is typical of working woman of coastal France.

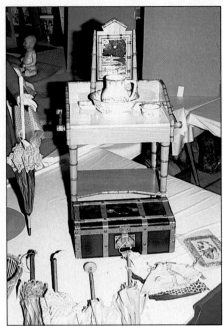

Accessories for sale by doll dealer.

Sweet innocent expression is almost childlike. Doll has swivel head, blue eyes and delicate painting.

We believe a doll in *original condition* wearing an *original costume* is an important find. *Quality* is also very important. A doll must exhibit fine, high-quality workmanship. To us, *beauty* is of great importance. We want a doll that is appealing. Other collectors might disagree—many prefer a doll with character or special features. For investment purposes, we feel quality and beauty are equal.

In all dolls, *markings* are important. With French fashion dolls, markings are less important because so many dolls were unmarked.

There are other things that make lady dolls good investments. Dolls with special historic value, because of their costuming or the fact they were owned by someone special, makes them important. Dolls with rare bodies, those of a special size, ethnic dolls or Portrait dolls are valuable. Sometimes dolls that are a part of a very special collection, such as fortunetelling dolls or a family of dolls or those that complete a collection, are good investments. They must be of authentic quality and esthetically pleasing.

We once advised collectors a doll must be perfect, or nearly perfect, to be investment quality. Now, with the same number of antique dolls being passed from collector to collector and from generation to generation, we have changed our minds. We feel some of these precious, lovely old dolls may be lost because they have a chip or hairline crack. This must *not* happen! These dolls must be preserved for future collectors.

Usually when a collection is sold, it brings more money and is better advertised if it contains a few special dolls. Sometimes a very unique doll will bring bidders to an auction. Other types of dolls may bring higher prices, such as those that are well-known, ones that have received ribbons at UFDC conventions, dolls that have been photographed for books or plates, or dolls that have been written up in magazine articles.

INVESTING IN FRENCH FASHION DOLLS

In this section, we provide information on different French fashion dolls so you can see how prices have changed over the past few decades.

Right: Doll marked *F* is 13 inches tall and will intrigue any collector. She has swivel neck and fine blond-mohair wig. Her wood body is fully articulated—even at waist, ankles and wrists. Dress is dark-green silk-taffeta, trimmed with tiny pleats of same fabric at hem and train. Full sleeves, apron front, boatneck and draped back are outlined in gold-threaded lace. This is fine example of couturier costume. Doll wears gold watch at her neck. She came with trunk, extra clothes and many accessories. Doll is also shown on page 128.

Fashion-Doll Collectors **109**

DOLL DESCRIPTION & PRICE LIST FROM JULY 1955

French fashion, 15 inches $75
Swivel shoulder head of pale bisque. New brown human-hair wig. Stationary gray-blue, blown-glass eyes; rimmed with black. Closed mouth; pierced ears. Dress of white brocade-taffeta printed with flowers.

French fashion, 25 inches $125
Rare flanged-neck doll of pale bisque. New brown human-hair wig. Stationary blue, feathered, blown-glass eyes. Closed mouth; ears unpierced. Hinged kid body. Tiny chip on edge of neck has been repaired. Dress of velvet and moire in two shades of blue with train and big pouf.

Rare doll, 13-1/2 inches $65
Swivel head of pale bisque. New brown human-hair wig. Blue blown-glass eyes. Ears unpierced. Body and legs of composition, with big feet that allow doll to stand alone. Lower arms and hands of bisque—tips of two fingers on each hand damaged but barely noticeable. When doll's back is pressed, she turns her head, throws up arms and squeaks. Wears copy of original dress—blue taffeta trimmed with white rickrack. Original hat trimmed with pearls.

French fashion, 17-1/2 inches $145
Swivel shoulder head of pale bisque. Original dark-brown wig. Stationary gray-blue, blown-glass eyes; pupils rimmed with black. Closed mouth; pierced ears. Wood body and limbs jointed at knees, hips, wrists, elbows and shoulders. Joints swivel at thighs and upper arms. Two fingers and four toes have been repaired. One pupil is larger than the other. Slight pale spot on one cheek. Wears white taffeta skirt and lavender jacket; original hat.

Fortuneteller, 13 inches $65
Stationary shoulder head of pale bisque. Original blond wig. Painted blue eyes. Closed mouth; pierced ears. Stiff kid body has mitten hands. Original, elaborate dress of red velvet and yellow satin is trimmed with lace and braid. Skirt hides red and black fortunetelling papers. Doll is attached to wood stand. With pointed hat, overall height is 20 inches.

French fashion, 17-1/2 inches $140
Swivel shoulder head of bisque. New brown wig. Stationary blue, feathered, blown-glass eyes. Closed mouth; pierced ears. Wood body jointed at knees, hips, elbows and shoulders. Redressed in lavender-and-white striped satin with lavender velvet bolero. Original hat of lavender faille trimmed with ribbon.

French fashion, 14 inches $75
Swivel shoulder head of bisque. Original blond Tibetan goat-hair wig. Stationary pale-blue, blown-glass eyes rimmed with darker blue. Closed mouth; pierced ears. Hinged kid body. Redressed in black taffeta trimmed with velvet-ribbon bows and black lace. Original blue bonnet made of blue taffeta, ribbon, tulle and flowers. Arms and hands are soiled; wires have rusted through fingers on right hand.

French fashion, 17 inches $115
Swivel shoulder head of pale bisque. New brown wig. Stationary deep-blue, threaded-glass eyes. Closed mouth; pierced ears. Hinged kid body. Wears original dress of black taffeta, with lavender stripes, and straw bonnet. Shoulders marked *E.B.*

On the opposite page, we have included a description and the asking price of some dolls in 1955. Prices include packing, crating in a wood box, insurance and shipment from France to the United States. These descriptions came with photos of dolls Philippe D'Albert-Lake (Antique Dolls, 5 Rue Dupont des Loges, Paris) wanted to sell. This type of advertising was, and is, often used by dealers. Photographs, descriptions and prices were, and still are, sent to prospective customers.

In studying the descriptions, we learned some wigs were changed, and some dolls were redressed. We also discovered fortunetelling dolls had a skirt over their fortunes. Our doll does not have an overskirt now. The fortuneteller doll listed here sold for $85 in 1955—we paid $1,250 for a similar doll in 1984. Both dolls are the same size. This is not a popular doll today and did not increase in value as much as some dolls.

HOW TO FIND FRENCH FASHION DOLLS

We know there are French fashion dolls still hidden away in trunks and attics. If you're a beginning collector without capital and you want to start collecting fashion dolls, try the following ideas first. Begin with your family, and ask if anyone has dolls. Often family members are glad someone is interested in their collection, and they're happy their dolls will have a safe home and proper care. Try your family and your husband's family, then ask friends and neighbors.

A small advertisement in the local newspaper may help you find a fashion doll at a reasonable price. Sometimes members of doll clubs will sell a doll at a lower price to help a new collector get started.

If you've collected modern, plastic or composition dolls, sell some and buy one fine fashion doll. If you're a doll maker, make a special doll or two to trade for a lady doll. Sell reproduction dolls to earn enough money. Sometimes selling a few pieces of doll furniture will bring enough money to buy a Parisienne.

Auctions are a good source of less-expensive lady dolls. Fashion dolls without clothing are always *much* lower in price than dressed ones. Absentee bidding is inexpensive for these dolls.

Finding French fashion dolls is not a problem for an advanced collector who attends doll shows, conventions and other meetings. They are among the most plentiful dolls; finding a rare doll or a fine costume is difficult.

Museum Closings—Another way to find exceptionally fine dolls is the closing of a small, privately owned doll museum. These museums are often closed after an owner dies, and no one wants to continue the museum. Collections are sometimes sold privately or at small estatelike auctions, rather than big doll auctions that are well-advertised.

Doll Dealers—Probably the best way to find good fashion dolls is through doll dealers. You can purchase dolls by mail as well as at shows. Most dealers have a 3-day return privilege and are glad to help you with special requests.

There are many doll dealers in the business of buying and selling dolls. Most dealers carry a variety of dolls, and occasionally some have French fashion dolls. Many dealers buy and sell only high-quality dolls and usually carry French dolls. You can locate various dealers by reading advertisements in doll magazines and by talking to people at doll shows and conventions. Also see the dealer list we include, beginning on page 137.

Try to get to know—by telephone, letter or in person—a few of the best doll dealers. One may call you if he or she has a doll you're looking for. Many times they do this before they advertise the doll. You may pay a little more for the doll when you buy it through a dealer, but you're able to locate a doll you would never find another way.

For one of our books, almost all the small French dolls (Milettes) were collected this way. We collect almost entirely by telephone and deal only with reliable dealers. They know the quality we seek so we seldom need to return a doll.

When we buy dolls by telephone or through dealers, we ask questions to help us. We always ask: "Are there any cracks or repairs?" "What are the markings?" "May we have a 3-day return privilege?" We can usually tell if a doll is the one we're looking for by the description. Sometimes a dealer who sends us a doll will include another doll for us to examine.

Within 3 days, we return a doll if we don't want it, if it isn't exactly as described or if it has something wrong with it. We also return a doll if we don't like it. It's all right to do this if you don't overdo it. We pay shipping charges when we return a doll.

Friends and Other Collectors—Buying dolls from friends or other collectors is another way to find good dolls—usually at fair prices. We

Fashion doll waiting to be purchased.

believe show expenses are added to the price of a doll.

At a show or convention, you can go from table to table and compare prices and dolls. Usually a dealer will let you examine a doll before you buy it. If there is anything wrong with the doll, have it noted in writing on the bill the seller gives you. Use the description below as an example:

1 Jumeau, fashion, 18 inches, $2,000. Hairline behind left ear. Costume original.

Auctions—Going to auctions to buy dolls is a fun, educational way to pass time. You can see more dolls and find out more about them in less time than any other way we know. If you're a new collector, you must be properly prepared for the event. If you aren't, you may experience difficulties.

We advise you to leave your money home the first few times you go to an auction. Use the time to learn how an auction operates, and study the dolls. In later auctions, follow these steps:

1. Purchase the doll catalog as soon as it is available (weeks before the auction). It usually costs between $10 and $15. Put your name on the auction mailing list so you'll be notified of upcoming sales.

2. Study the catalog. Mark any French fashions you're interested in. Learn everything you can about them *before* the auction by studying books and price guides.

3. Learn the catalog system of how dolls are written up. The aim of the catalog makers is to present the doll so it will bring the highest price. The picture and writeup are used to sell the doll.

4. Check to see what similar dolls have sold for. Mark your highest bid in your own code in your catalog. (For more information on codes, see our book *Doll Collecting for Fun & Profit,* also published by HPBooks.)

5. On the day of the auction, go early so you have plenty of time to look. Concentrate on dolls you marked in your book. If necessary, change the bids in your catalog *after* studying the dolls. Ask the attendants any questions you may have.

6. Establish credit by signing in with the auction house. This lets them know how you will pay for any dolls you purchase.

7. Don't discuss your plans to bid (what or how much) with anyone except your family.

8. Decide your bid and the total you have allowed for the auction. *Do not go over this amount!*

suggest both parties consult price guides or find out what the doll sold for at the most-recent auction. Be aware that price guides are only general, and auction people take 30% of the selling price.

Usually a doll bought from a friend, original owner or collector will cost much less because there is no dealer markup, advertising charge or show expense. Sometimes the quality of a doll, her condition or her costume are so much finer than you could get at an auction that you are willing to pay more. Be your own judge, but study the doll carefully. If you buy a doll from an original owner and she is unaware of its value, pay a fair price. It can take away the joy of collecting if you cheat someone.

Doll Shows and Conventions—Buying dolls at a doll show or convention may be the easiest, safest, way to buy dolls. Sales rooms at conventions and shows are well-controlled, and dealers want to protect their names so they can get into the next sale or convention. Some buyers think they get the fairest price at a show where there is a lot of competition for buyers. Other buyers

SELLING PRICES OF FRENCH FASHION DOLLS

Below are auction and convention selling prices for French fashion dolls from May 1983 through January 1985. Original costumes are listed; other costumes are not. Complete information on each doll was not available. If not marked *shoulder head*, the doll had a swivel head.

HEIGHT/MARKING	DESCRIPTION	COSTUME	SELLING PRICE
10 inches *A Smiler*	Kid body		$ 800
11 inches *FB-3/0*		Original	900
12 inches *FG-0*			975
12 inches *FG 3/0*	Shoulder head		300
13 inches	Kid body	Original	1300
13 inches *B Smiler*	Kid body		1400
13 inches *C Smiler*	Kid body		1300
14 inches *EB*	Kid body	Original	1200
15 inches *F Smiler*	Kid body		1500
15 inches *B-Jne CIE*		Original	1550
16 inches *E Smiler*	Kid body		1600
16 inches	Body stamped *Mme. Rohmer*	Original	950
16 inches	Body stamped *Simonne*		1050
16 inches	Shoulder head kid body; bisque hands		700
17 inches	Body stamped *Simonne*		1800
17 inches *3 Jumeau*	Bisque arms		4000
17 inches *FG*	Kid body; chipped ear	Original	1237
17 inches *8*	Kid body; bisque hands	Original	375
17 inches *FG-4*	Bisque hands and feet		1500
17 inches *FG-3*		Original	1200
17-3/4 inches *4 Jumeau*			4000
18 inches	Body stamped *Simonne*		2200
18 inches *4 Jumeau*	Kid body	Original	1320
18 inches	Kid-over-wood body; bisque hands and feet	Original	2750
18 inches	Kid body; gusseted shoulder head; bald head; minor eye chip	Original	425
18 inches *FG-4*	Gesland body		2300
18 inches *FG-4*	Painted eyes; shoulder head		750
19 inches *FG-5*	Replaced new body		950
21-1/4 inches	Kid body	Original; 8 hats and extra clothing	2523
22 inches *9 Jumeau*			3000
25 inches *Portrait*	Kid body		2450
26 inches	Body signed *Jumeau*		3250
27 inches *FG-10*			2650
28 inches *FG-9*	Kid body; hairline crack on head		1500
28 inches *FG-10*			3200
28-1/2 inches *10 Jumeau*	Kid body	Original	2600

PRICES OF DOLLS SHOWING INFLUENCE OF BODY MATERIAL

Body materials influence the selling price, as shown below. Prices from May 1983 to January 1985.

HEIGHT/MARKINGS	TYPE OF BODY	COSTUME	SELLING PRICE
14 inches	Muslin		$ 500
16 inches *FG-3*	Wood		2000
16 inches	Wood; bisque arms; dowel joints		2500
16 inches	Gesland		1500
16 inches	Wood; full articulation	Original	3000
17 inches	Wood	Original	2090
17 inches	Kid-over-wood bisque arms; swivel waist	Extra clothes	2500
17 inches	Kid-over-wood; stamped *Simonne*		2000
17 inches *FG-3*	Gesland		1800
18 inches *FG-4*	Wood		2400
18 inches	Wood; shoulder head		1700
19 inches	Wood		2300
23 inches	Kid-over-wood	Original with trunk & trousseau	2500
38 inches *FG* in scroll	Gesland	Original	3300
12 inches	Leather; unjointed	Original	400
12 inches	Leather		800
13 inches *Jumeau*	Leather		875
14 inches *Jumeau*	Leather		1000
15 inches	Leather	Original	1000
15 inches *E.B.*	Leather	Original, with trunk & trousseau	2750
17 inches *Bru*	Leather	Original	2750
19 inches *FG*	Leather	Antique clothes	2950
22 inches	Leather; individually sewn fingers	Bonnet & original costume	1750
26 inches *FG*	Leather; shoulder head		1430

EXPANDING YOUR DOLL KNOWLEDGE

There are many ways to expand your doll knowledge. The more you learn about the dolls, the better your collection will be. And you'll be a better-informed collector. We feel these ideas are not only for the novice but also for skilled collectors.

Visit Museums—Make a trip to a museum you have been wanting to visit. See pages 138 to 141 for a list of museums in the United States.

Give yourself time to study the dolls on display. Some museums have reference rooms; others have curators that will share their knowledge with you. Check to see if doll books are sold in the museum shop. Buy any you need to add to your doll-book collection.

Seeing rare dolls at a museum helps train your eye to recognize different dolls. It helps place dolls in their proper place in history, and it can help with costuming.

Join Doll Clubs—Join a doll club, preferably one associated with the UFDC. Join an active club that studies old dolls. Share with members your knowledge and collection in exchange for other people's expertise and experience.

There are many advantages to membership, such as a club's magazine, conventions, workshops, classes, lectures and other special activities. One of the greatest benefits of conventions is the number of collectors you meet from all over the world.

Learn from Dolls—In hobbies, we hear the term

SIZES OF FASHION DOLLS

Size numbers and letters of French fashion dolls can vary with a maker, but they also vary with the type of body. In some bodies the stuffing expanded, the body became warped, then became shorter. This can change the total height of the doll by as much as an inch. We searched through 300 dolls and doll records to make some sense out of the numbered markings found on dolls.

Heads Marked F.G. — Below is all we found for heads marked *F.G.* on leather bodies.

F.G. 2/0 — 9 inches
    3/0 — 11 inches
    0 — 12 inches
    1 — 13 inches
    2 — 15 inches
    3 — 17 inches
    4 — 18 inches
    5 — 19 inches
    6 — 22 inches
    7 & 8 were not found
    9 — 25 inches
    10 — 28 inches

Other Marked Dolls — A head marked with a number and a body signed *Jumeau* are listed below. We found two sizes:

    9 — 22 inches
    11 — 26 inches

Smilers — Below are some sizes we found for Smilers. Faces are found on different bodies, so heights can vary with the type of body.

    A — 10 inches
    B — 13 inches
    C — 13 inches
    D — 15 inches
    E — 16 inches
    E — 17 inches
    F — 17 inches

Note: B and C are same size; E and F are same size.

Numbered Heads — These, on articulated wood bodies, could be Bru, Jumeau or Gesland. We found the following sizes:

    1 — 13 inches
    2 — 15 inches
    3 — 17 inches
    4 — 19 inches

Portrait heads are unmarked. Larger dolls are usually 20 to 34 inches tall. Unmarked heads on stamped Simonne bodies have no letters or numbers; bodies are from 16 to 20 inches tall.

We still find contradictions to the above listings. Many dolls have had their heads changed, and there are things we still don't know. But this gives you a general idea of sizes.

"hands-on experience." In doll collecting, nothing can compare with hands-on work with dolls. Combine studies with hands-on experience.

Attend doll shows — it's an entertaining, educational way to see a wide variety of dolls from all periods of time. Examine displays, and study doll faces. Ask questions. Dealers usually are delighted to answer questions and explain quality and condition of the dolls.

Read Doll Literature — Subscribe to several doll periodicals, and read them thoroughly. They are excellent sources of up-to-date information on many kinds of dolls. Magazines also contain news of doll shows, exhibits and other things of interest. Some contain advertisements for dolls. Magazines can keep you abreast of collecting trends and prices.

Buy some new doll books, and read them. You'll find many excellent general books and books on specific types of dolls, price guides and doll histories. Knowledge is important for successful doll collecting. A shelf of doll books is a good reference tool.

Take Classes — Take a seminar or class on old dolls. These are not easy to find, but doll clubs often have members or know dealers who, for a fee, will hold a lesson or series of lessons. We do this periodically for a small group of collectors. This also can be hands-on experience.

In our seminars, we often show how an old doll was made. It's also helpful to make a doll. Doll studios are located in many towns and cities. Hands-on experience will instill in you an appreciation for antique dolls and their creators.

Appraise Your Collection—Have your collection appraised. Professional doll appraisals are important for insuring, selling or giving dolls to family members. If no professional appraiser is near you, use our book, *How to Collect French Bébé Dolls*, also published by HPBooks, for a guide to do-it-yourself appraisals.

Check doll clubs near you for a qualified appraiser. The following nationally known antique appraisers also have people who appraise dolls:

American Society of Appraisers
Dulles International Airport
P.O. Box 17265
Washington D.C. 20041
(703) 620-3838

The Appraisers Association of America
60 E. 42nd St.
New York, NY 10165
(212) 867-9775

The International Society of Appraisers
424 W. Washington Blvd.
Chicago, IL 60606
(312) 867-2480.

Work With Your Own Collection—Study your collection, and make a better display of the dolls you have. Proper cleaning, display and storage are essential to maintain even a small collection. Often, undressing a doll you may have had for years reveals a mark or identification point you missed before. This was true for us when we began studying French fashion dolls we had accumulated over a 15-year period. We discovered many new and interesting facts about our French fashion dolls.

DOLL IDEAS AND SUGGESTIONS

Below are some ideas and suggestions for collectors of French fashion dolls. These tips can help you become a more-knowledgeable, successful doll collector.

1. Don't swap dolls with anyone. It's never an even swap. Whether consciously or not, one person will take advantage of the other, and swapper's remorse may set in. Friendship is more important than a doll.
2. Realize when buying dolls from dealers that many dealers are first collectors and second sellers. Most collectors keep the best dolls for themselves.
3. Sell a rare doll of unestablished value through an auction house. If they advertise it properly, the doll will sell for the highest price.
4. Watch for fraud when you lack comparison on extremely rare dolls. It's easier to defraud someone on a rare doll than on a known doll.
5. Develop your own appreciation of dolls so you'll have the courage to make your own judgments and buy what you like.
6. Use a strong light or a black light inside a bisque head. It will help locate cracks and repairs.
7. Be careful not to be influenced by the bonnet a doll wears or her pretty dress when buying. Judge the doll from the *inside* out. But remember, there is no substitute for an original costume, and a doll in original clothing is worth more.
8. Many things influence the value and desirability of a doll, including:
   - Historical significance.
   - Maker.
   - If the doll is part of a series.
   - If the doll is needed to complete a group.
   - Where the doll was made.
   - Variations of molds.
9. Learn the differences between investment and speculation in dolls. *Investment* means buying dolls to keep for a long time, with the expectation they will increase in value. *Speculation* means buying and selling dolls quickly for profit.
10. Understand that people are involved in investment and speculation all the time. Dealers at an auction speculate on the dolls they buy—except for the dolls they add to their own collection. Usually dealers buy less-expensive dolls and make a quick profit to cover the cost of a better doll for their own collection.
11. Collectors buy for long-term investment. Auction houses buy solely for speculation.
12. Display fashion dolls to give them a new dimension. They were originally toys, but they are also sculptures of charming ladies. They can become centers of interest in the proper decor.
13. Preserve any history if it is known, and keep it with the doll. Each doll has a special story to

---

Left: Closeup of lady in lavender, also shown on page 22 and cover. Doll was in a museum for many years, which explains superb condition of her hat, dress and hair. She has swivel neck, and head is pressed. Eyebrows are thin, arched and very light. Eyelashes are pale charcoal. Eyes are light-blue paperweight, with darker rim around iris. Lips are two-toned. Blond-mohair wig is still in original style; hat may never have been removed. Ignore mildew spotting on costume.

tell about her history and her many owners.

Doll collecting is habit-forming. You say you have had enough and must not collect another doll—but you will. The lure of the find often breaks the will of a collector.

SHARING AND EXHIBITING FRENCH FASHION DOLLS

You will enjoy your hobby more if you share your dolls with others who have a common interest. In the past, one has been able to share the experience of collecting Parisiennes only with advanced collectors. Other collectors have lacked the know-how to collect and fully appreciate these dolls. When we go to doll conventions, French fashions on exhibit are usually owned by long-time collectors or dealers.

Fashion dolls are not easy to transport to shows or conventions. Clothing is fragile. You must decide how to share your dolls. Some collectors realize clothing will only last a certain length of time—it's better to share the dolls and deal with the problem of deteriorated clothing when it occurs.

Traveling with Dolls—You can ship fashion dolls by air in trunks without too much fear of breaking. Wrap breakable heads, hands and feet in plastic bubble paper. Stuff gowns with tissue paper to keep them from being crushed. A plastic bag over the entire doll keeps the gown and hair in shape.

If you're going to take one or two dolls with you on a plane, wrap them as described above. Put the doll in a slightly larger box, and carry her aboard the plane. We have carried as many as four dolls without difficulty.

Local exhibits are easier on dolls. We occasionally set up exhibits in a library or bank. Exhibit your dolls *only* in locked, glass cases.

We are often asked to set up a table of dolls when we give a lecture. This is unsafe, and we never do it! Costumes of French fashion dolls will not stand people pinching and feeling them nor will the doll wigs stand pulling.

We display our dolls in our home. We don't let just anyone see our collection, but with an appointment and identification from a doll club, we will show our dolls. We feel it's good to share our dolls. Often doll-club people have knowledge they share with us, or sometimes they bring a doll for us to see. Sharing usually works both ways.

If you have a fine collection and live in fear each time you leave your home, collecting isn't worth it. Protect your dolls the best you can, then relax and live your life. Dolls should not be a burden or a constant worry.

Share dolls with photos and slides. You can see in this book that other collectors have shared their dolls and their knowledge with us, and we have passed this along to you.

Left: 13-inch unmarked, swivel-headed doll is stamped *Simonne* on body. Flat-shaped ears are pierced. Eyes are old, flat and cobalt-blue. Leather body is fully gusseted. Doll has no toes; fingers and thumbs are indicated by stitching. Doll has well-styled, blond-mohair wig over cork pate. She wears original couturier fashion dress in blue-green iridescent silk-taffeta. Jacket and skirt are hand-bound and trimmed with ruffles. Buttons are cut steel and seem too large for doll. She wears antique lace shawl. Blue flowers have been added to hair. Lace-up boots have gold bow and buckle on toe.

Pulling It Together

French fashion dolls and their exquisite costumes are not easy to preserve. Collectors want to enjoy them, yet dolls and costumes must be preserved. If we wrap a doll and her costume in white sheeting and store her in a cedar chest, everything would probably last longer. But there is little enjoyment in having a collection stored in trunks. French fashion dolls must be in view where they can be enjoyed every day.

PROTECTING YOUR DOLLS

If you stop to consider the things that are bad for a doll and her clothing, there are steps you can take to protect her. After purchasing a doll, most collectors undress it to see what they have purchased or have the doll undressed before they buy it. This procedure, when done in haste, is one of the *worst* things you can do to a fragile, 100-year-old costume.

Many fine fabrics, such as silk and silk-taffeta, crack when a doll is undressed. It's better to look gently under clothing on dolls that have never been undressed. Other types of dolls can be undressed, then dressed again when purchased. But with French fashion dolls, there is no easy way to take fragile garments off without the fabric cracking or breaking. The costume is very important. We have many lady dolls in our collection that have never been undressed.

Air pollutants cause fine fabrics to deteriorate. Pollutants also affect other natural materials on these dolls, such as leather, paper, wood, animal hair and body fillers. We believe car exhaust, cigarette and other smoke, salt from sea air and sulphurs from manufacturing plants are the worst.

Natural and artificial light are also hard on fabrics and materials. Both types of lighting are damaging because they fade fabrics.

Dampness can cause mold, warping or shrinking of fabrics and bodies. Dryness causes cracking and brittleness of fabric bodies and leather

Left: 18-inch, all-original Parisienne wrapped in a Paisley shawl. These shawls were especially woven in miniature for dolls and were made in Paisley, Scotland. Her red-and-black wool skirt is pleated away from inverted box pleat in the front. Bodice is of same material; it is tightly fitted. Neck and sleeves are edged in white lace. Bonnet is ruffled and trimmed with flowers. She wears watch, brooch and tiny pearls. Doll is marked 0.

bodies. Rapid changes in temperatures and humidity levels may also damage fragile materials.

Insects can harm natural materials; they are worse in the southern part of the United States. But the northern part of the United States must deal with clothes moths and museum beetles.

There are some things you can do to handle pests and other problems. First, it's better not to overcrowd fashion dolls when you display them in your home. Dolls and fabrics need space to hang and breathe.

It's also best to keep dolls in a glass cabinet with tight-fitting doors. Antique or modern glass domes are good for controlling atmosphere around a doll. Some new glass cases, with mirrors in the back, are made in many sizes to fit a particular-size doll. Glass cases are square, oblong or hexagonal. Cases are good protection against insects and changes in atmospheric conditions, such as heat and moisture.

Don't place open dolls, doll cases or domes in direct sunlight. Keep them out of direct line of a window where sun comes in. Artificial light can also be damaging, such as cases with lighting fixtures very close to dolls. Do not leave lights on for long periods because the case will heat up, and the heat dries things out.

You *can* help preserve costumes. Wash and iron cotton clothing. Place white tissue paper under fragile skirts to change the position of draping. Stand a doll that has been sitting so materials don't fade in one place or crack. Dolls that are close together can be spaced farther apart.

Protect dolls dressed in wool, or those with wool petticoats, from moths and other insects. The best protection we've found is a 1-inch-wide piece of No-Pest Strip. When using a strip, be sure it doesn't touch costume fabric. We have glass shelves, so we lay the strip on the shelf. It can also be placed in a small open box or in a glass. The strip will last up to 6 months with no offensive odor.

Don't place a new doll in a cabinet as soon as you bring her home. If possible, take time to undress the doll carefully, and inspect clothing for moths. Check the hair to see if insects have caused damage. Lady dolls and their costumes

Hoops worn by Bru fashion doll with wood body.

are mostly made of natural materials, which is easily damaged by insects.

After close inspection, if there are signs of damage, put the doll and some moth crystals in a paper bag. Close the bag, seal it and leave it for several days. Occasionally move the bag gently to stir the fumes inside—you want to be sure fumes get to *all* parts of the doll. When you remove the doll from the bag, it is safe to put her in your cabinet. It's easier to take precautions and *not* introduce insects into the cabinet than it is to get rid of them once they begin to multiply.

Every collector must do all within his or her power to protect a collection. Don't pack your dolls away where you can't enjoy them. After you have done what you can, stop worrying.

EXHIBITING DOLLS

People exhibit their dolls for many reasons, such as at UFDC competitions for educational purposes, at state fairs and doll shows for ribbons or at libraries and banks for the enjoyment of others.

Right: Corners of mouth on this Smiler are drawn in more than on other dolls. Doll has same type of eyelids and double chin. Head is pressed, and ears are pierced through lobe. Eyes are unusual—iris is gray with outer rim of blue to give effect of green eyes. Eyebrows are deep tan and nicely arched. Eyelashes are gray. She wears reproduction hat to match dress. Parts and decorations were taken from antique hat. Doll is also shown on page 83.

Exhibiting dolls is educational for you and for the people who will view and enjoy the exhibit. When dolls are entered in competitions, you may be surprised at what you learn from judges and owners of other dolls in the same class. When we exhibit our dolls, there are many pleasant benefits, including making new friends, finding new dolls and learning new facts about our dolls.

Exhibiting French fashion dolls, either near your home or in some distant city, is hard on a doll. Transporting dolls can be one of the worst things you can do to a fine French costume. Yet as doll collectors, we must do our part for others so they may enjoy our dolls. We believe it's worth an extra crack in the taffeta or a few more wrinkles or even a little sawdust sifting out to exhibit a fine doll. It's the best way to share dolls and knowledge. It is part of the joy of collecting.

To a lesser degree, sharing can occur in your home. Some collectors open their homes to doll clubs and members. We allow doll clubs to visit us—we try to help collectors by holding seminars. We take our dolls off their shelves and out from under their domes. Occasionally we undress a doll so guests can have firsthand information about a body or particular joint. In this way, we help others and preserve and pass along our knowledge.

Doll collectors must practice the same rules of courtesy as everyone else. *Never drop in on a collector*—always make an appointment in advance. Many collectors are busy people.

We realize sharing our dolls is wear and tear on them, but we believe it is part of being a responsible collector. There are instances when this type of sharing should not be done, and doll-club members understand why we don't undress a doll or allow photos to be taken. For example, we don't undress some of our French fashion dolls that have never been undressed because the costumes wouldn't stand it.

Other collectors also have shared their collections with us. We were visiting Lenore Thomas, who has one of the finest doll collections we know of, and she offered to undress a French fashion doll with one of the rarest bodies known to collectors. We are grateful because it gave us an opportunity to see the body, which we would not have seen except for her generosity. She also let us take pictures of it. See pages 56 and 57. This encouraged us to write this book to share our knowledge and the knowledge others have shared with us.

REPAIRING FRENCH FASHION DOLLS

Many French fashion dolls have leather bodies or leather torsos. Bodies were filled with many things, including ground cork, horsehair, bran, cotton, wool, sawdust or other mixtures. Because of their age, French fashion dolls often leak filling in various places. Leaking must be stopped and slack places filled. If arms, legs or hands are missing, replace them with old ones or reproduction parts.

Sometimes lady bodies are stuffed so tight they're ready to explode. Occasionally, a hip seam pops. These conditions are caused by sawdust absorbing moisture and expanding. Other fillers also absorb moisture. Occasionally we find lady bodies as limp as rags, with most of the stuffing gone. When possible, repair a body instead of replacing it.

When you buy or receive a doll, keep everything. Keep the old cork pate and the wig, if possible. Badly broken shoulderplates are impossible to replace, so glue them together—they usually won't show when a doll is dressed.

If there are small spots where a doll body is leaking stuffing and needs filling, you can usually fill the space with dacron stuffing, which is available at most sewing-supply stores. Stuff the hole until it is tight, then double-patch the leaking spot. Old leather is almost impossible to sew because it tears so easily. It's easier to make a double patch.

Making a Double Patch—First, trim the hole in the body so it is neat. Next, cut a piece of old, white, glove leather larger than the hole. Carefully work the patch *under* the hole so it's flat.

After the glove leather is worked under the hole in the body, use rubber cement around and under the edge of the old leather to hold the patch in place. Apply the cement, and let it dry a little. Then cover the entire area and 1/8 inch of the body, beyond the hole, with rubber cement. Cut another patch of glove leather that is larger than the repaired hole by 1/8 inch. Apply the patch, and let it dry. The larger the doll, or the

Left: We purchased this shoulder head, marked *F3G,* for this book. She has straight-legged leather body. She is the only painted-eye F.G. doll we have seen. Her costume is black silk with fitted bodice. Skirt is full in back with train.

larger the hole, the farther the patch must extend onto the body.

Sometimes, it's better to try to sew the seam, then cut another clean hole to add stuffing.

Too Much Stuffing—In places where stuffing has expanded, cut a round hole in the hip, upper legs or lower legs to remove some filler. Double patch the spot using the same method as described above. Use the piece you removed as the top patch. Use a sharp knife or scalpel to cut a round hole in the body. A more-detailed description of this procedure can be found in our book *Doll Collecting for Fun & Profit*, also published by HPBooks.

Missing Pieces—Missing arms and legs are almost impossible to replace. It's important to try to find an old replacement part. At doll conventions and doll shows, some dealers sell old parts. If you can't find an old replacement part, buy reproduction parts. We feel it's better to replace *both* hands or feet, even if only one is missing, so they match. You must decide for yourself if you want an old or new foot or hand.

Reproduction Bodies—Try to preserve precious old bodies. When all else fails, or there is no body, we recommend a reproduction leather body. Buy the best body available, or study body making and make your own.

Caring for and Preserving Leather Bodies—Leather bodies may be in good shape except finger seams are open (unsewn), and some filling is missing. Fingers need gentle handling.

Repair fingers with a darning needle. Carefully push some dacron into the finger, then stitch it closed with a small needle. Don't pull thread too tight because it may cause the leather to rip. Sometimes it's better to use rubber cement to glue the finger closed than to try to sew it.

Many lady dolls had kid arms that were left unstuffed at the shoulder. They were tucked under the shoulderplate. These arms are often well-worn and have lost sawdust. Sometimes a little white glue around the leak can stop it without having to take the doll apart. At other times, you must remove the shoulderplate and find the source of the problem.

Many leather bodies were lined with muslin, which was closed at the top and sewn. The shoulderplate was fastened on top of this muslin sack. If muslin is torn or unsewn, it can cause a stream of sawdust to come out of the doll every time she is moved.

Never use adhesive tape on a leather body. Tape does not age well and makes a worse spot than the one you had. It's better not to repair bodies with cloth. Old kid or leather gloves are the best for body repairs, and they are still available.

Repairing Other Types of Bodies—Repairs to wood bodies and wood joints must be done by an experienced craftsman. Do *not* do it yourself unless you're sure you have the skill.

Patch cloth bodies with cloth. If possible, match the old material.

Clean bisque parts with a cloth or cotton swab dipped in commercial cleaner, such as 409. Don't get any liquid on leather or wood bodies because it will discolor the leather or wood.

FASTENING HEADS TO BODIES

French fashion dolls have a head, shoulderplate and body pieces. These three items were fastened together in many ways. We have opened up many dolls, and the method of fastening described below is the one used most often.

The bisque head has a wood ball. A large type of cotter pin goes down through the ball, through a piece of kid, through the neck and the kid-lined indentation of the shoulderplate, through another piece of kid, then through a conical spring and a tin washer.

The end of the cotter pin was bent over to hold the head tightly, but the arrangement allows the head to swivel. Holes in the shoulderplate are usually called *sew holes*, but originally the shoulderplate had nails pushed through the holes into the stuffing of the body.

Kid from the torso or a separate collarlike piece of kid was pulled up over the lower edges all around the shoulderplate. (When you have a shoulderplate off, always note any marks or numbers inside.)

In Jumeau fashion dolls, we usually find the arrangement is reversed. A regular spring (not conical) is used in the head, and the turned-over cotter pin is under the shoulderplate.

A spring in either the head or shoulderplate is necessary to make the head fit tightly. Shoulder

Right: 14-inch Jumeau doll marked *1:* and *J* is on wood body covered with kid. Fully lined gown is unusually full and draped in train in back. Fabric is shiny brown silk-taffeta with black stripe. Bottom of skirt has section of diagonal stripes with puffs and ruffles. Gold braid and gold cord circle skirt four times. Top is boat-necked, and sleeves are short, showing unusual wood arms. Bodice is fitted. Her brown flowered hat accents costume. Doll is also shown on page 26.

heads also were fastened with nails through the sew holes, and leather was glued around the edges of a shoulderplate. When repairing the head-spring arrangement, check automotive and hardware stores for washers and springs.

REPRODUCTION FRENCH FASHIONS

Reproduction dolls extend the life of a particular era of dolls. Many priceless old dolls could never be owned by general doll lovers, but a fine replica can be owned and enjoyed by many. Reproductions help evade the destructive impact of time.

We know little about the thoughts or plans of old doll makers—Bru, Jumeau, Schmitt—during the time they produced fashion dolls. We have studied the doll makers, their construction techniques, the materials they used, their flawless workmanship, painstaking skill and attention to detail. It is the results of their efforts that we prize today in fashion dolls. Their skills make antique dolls the beautiful pieces of art they are. These same skills are used today by doll makers who make our modern reproductions and original dolls.

The word *reproduction* does not mean inferior. Reproduction dolls, produced by some of our finest doll artists, are superior to antiques in several ways. Modern materials are finer. An artist studies until he or she has the traditional skills, materials and techniques to perfect her work. And modern artists complete an entire doll.

When you choose a reproduction doll, select the best. Studying dolls and doll making will contribute to your awareness. The beautiful reproduction dolls will become heirlooms. Poor reproduction dolls will fall by the wayside.

FABRICS OF THE PAST

An authentic copy of an old fabric is known as a *document*. In seeking to re-create a historically accurate costume for a French fashion doll,

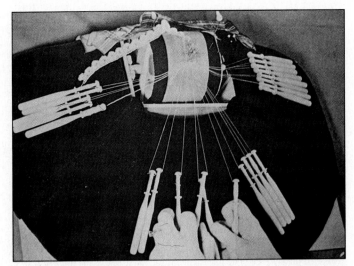
Complicated process of making bobbin lace.

use documentary fabrics when possible. These fabrics were once difficult to find, but today they are becoming more available. Fabrics are now available for the era of the fashion doll, from 1850 to 1870, and also the later Victorian and Art-Nouveau periods. To be accurate, a costumer must know the year, within a 10-year period, if he or she wishes to re-create a costume.

New fabrics are machine-made, so texture and colors do not exactly duplicate old handmade fabric. But the new re-created fabrics are so much like originals that we cannot complain. Today's fabrics are made with chemical dyes that do not fade or soften as much as old vegetable dyes. Antique fabrics were printed with wood blocks or copper plates or were hand-engraved. Today's textiles are printed with steel rollers or photoengraving processes for speed and economy.

Documentary fabrics are created mostly for use by museums. Doll costumers must search for them in museum shops that sell fabric. Silk shops and some doll dealers import them from Europe. Re-created fabrics are not as available to the costumer as collectors would like.

Left: Smiler on jointed wood body is also shown on page 109. Doll has same-shaped mouth as other Smilers but with round face modeling and smaller double chin. Ears are pierced into pressed-bisque head. Doll's eyes are wide open, but heavy lid is indicated. Eyelashes are painted rather straight up, with heavier strokes. Eyebrows are many tiny lines of deep amber to match hair. Note tricolored eyes; they are sought by collectors.

Lace for French Fashion Costumes—There has been a revival in the appreciation of handmade laces. The art of making lace has been passed from generation to generation. Some antique needle laces and fine bobbin laces are still available. Dolls today still wear beautiful dresses, bonnets and underclothing trimmed with fine lace. Antique laces were made of cotton or silk. If you must use new lace, use only lace made of cotton.

Lace making has seen renewed interest, especially with doll makers. One group, the International Old Lacers, Inc., works to keep the art alive. They hold a convention each year and exhibit their work in competition. They also sell their finished products and the items necessary to make lace. Classes are held to teach people how to make Bedfordshire, Bucks Point and Honiton lace.

Under the heading of laces, we include other handmade edgings, such as knitted lace, crocheted edgings, bobbin lace and needlepoint lace.

There are many types of lace, but those listed below are the ones seen and used most often by costume makers. Antique laces can still be found; certain areas, as New England, are best for searching for old lace.

Medallion Lace—Separate motifs that can be any shape. These pieces are usually inserted into fabric.

Galloon Lace—Wide lace with a scallop on both edges. Often has metallic threads.

Insertion Lace—Both edges of this type of lace are straight. Lace is sewn between two pieces of fabric or other lace.

Beading Lace—Lace with holes for running ribbon through. It is usually a type of insertion lace.

Edging Lace—This type of lace has one straight edge and one decorative edge. It is used on bonnets, collars and cuffs as edging.

Matched underclothing of Gesland-bodied doll has lovely lace edging around hem.

Left: Couturier-dressed Bru is all original. Note soft shaping of bisque hands. Doll carries card case, lorgnette and parasol. Top of dress is sand-gray silk-taffeta with matching ruffles. Skirt is deep mauve satin, and back is bustled. Hat, with fine straw edging, is decorated with bows and minute flowers. She stands in Swedish shipyard.

Glossary

Applied Ears—Ears made in separate molds and put on greenware heads.

Articulated—Jointed.

Assembler—One who put doll parts together but did not make parts.

Bald Head—Head is solid on top, with no opening or pate.

Balmoral Boots—Low boots that lace up front.

Basque—Bodice that extends below waistline.

Bisque—Fired porcelain.

Cartouche—Scroll.

Cascades of Lace—Series of rows of gathered lace.

Character Faces—Dolls with unusual faces; sometimes Portrait dolls. Not usually found on French fashion dolls.

Chevé Silk—Silk that changes color when light reflects off it.

Coiffures—Hairstyles.

Couturier—Designer of ladies' fashions.

Crinoline—Petticoat of horsehair or cage of metal hoops, which holds skirt out in a circle.

Demitrain—Small train of fabric made from fullness of skirt in back.

Festoon—Wreath or garland of flowers.

Flanged Neck—Projecting rim or collar to hold head in place, guide it or attach it to shoulderplate. On one Rohmer fashion doll we found a shoulderplate with a flat rim around neck hole. Neck fits down on this, and head is held in place with wood dowel covered with leather. This is different from flanged, or flared-out, neck used on baby-doll heads.

Doll has beautiful paperweight eyes.

Flat Eyes—Glass eyes with *no* crystal over pupil. Older than paperweight eyes. Usually cobalt-blue.

Fraise—Frill of material or lace at neck.

Frill—Gathered ruffle.

Galloon—Wide lace with metallic threads.

Gimpe—Bodice worn under low-necked dress.

Greenware—Unfired porcelain.

Gussets—Oval patches of material added to joint sections to allow arm or leg to move.

Gutta-percha—Rubberlike substance from trees; used in 1880s to make doll bodies and sometimes heads.

Hairpin Lace—Lace made on hairpins.

Insertion Lace—Lace inserted into fabric.

Left: Closeup of F.G. doll shown on page 17. Bisque was poured, and ears were pierced through lobe. Gray paperweight eyes are lined with blue. Note formed lid above eye, fine black eyelashes and very thin brown eyebrows. Mouth is drawn in at corners, lightly painted and accented. Red-blond human-hair wig was probably replaced in the 1940s when she was added to a museum. Bonnet is black velvet with combination of faded feathers and still-bright flowers.

Keystone—Trapazoid shape stamped on some shoes.

Kid—Thin or split leather.

Leather—Animal skin.

Lawn—Fine cotton fabric.

Mannequins—Full-sized forms for displaying dresses.

Marseilles Cloth—Ribbed cotton material.

Milettes—French Bébé dolls under 14 inches tall.

Moiré—Watered silk.

Pandoras—Half-size mannequins or dolls used to display fashions.

Pannier—Overskirt draped at sides.

Pantalets—Undergarment worn by ladies or girls.

Pantaloons—Full underdrawers, gathered at ankle.

Paperweight Eyes—Glass eyes with clear crystal over pupil.

Pinking—Series of small points on fabric to prevent raveling; used instead of hand finishing.

Porcelain—Clay that fires or matures to translucent bisque.

Port-monnaie—Card case. Many French fashion costumes had pockets for card cases, and some fashion dolls carried cases.

Portrait Fashion Dolls—Dolls with unusual or realistic faces. They may have been modeled to look like real people.

Pouf—Gathered material that is puffed out.

Reticle—Handbag carried by drawstrings.

Ruching—Finely pleated edging used as trim on dresses and bonnets.

Sew Holes—Holes through lower edge of bisque shoulderplate or shoulder head. Originally nails were pushed through holes into stuffed body to hold head and shoulderplate on. On cloth bodies, holes were used to actually *sew* head to body.

Shades—Colors darkened with black.

Shoulder Head—Doll's head, neck and shoulder made in one piece. Head cannot be turned or moved. Sometimes called *stiff neck* by dealers.

Shoulderplate—Separate plate covering shoulder; used with swivel heads.

Smiler—Doll with "Mona Lisa" smile. Maker unknown.

Snood—Coarse net used over hair in back to

22-1/2-inch Smiler, incised *Déposé J* on forehead and *J* on back of head. She has articulated wood arms, and her torso and legs are kid. Front seam of her body curves under her tummy. She wears ermine pillbox hat and cape. Lenore Thomas doll.

keep it neat and in place.

Soutache—Braid used in 1860s to decorate garments.

Swivel Head—Doll's neck fits into hollow on shoulderplate that allows head to turn.

Tatting—Handmade edging.

Tints—Colors diluted with white.

Tricot—Knit material.

Trousseaus—Collection of clothing belonging to, or made for, one doll.

Unborn Lambskin Wig—Wig made of unborn lamb. Other wigs were made of sheepskin, mohair or human hair.

Left: Unmarked doll is dressed in simple, homemade country dress. Fabric is faded pale-green, hand-woven wool. Dress is simple, with low-cut neck outlined in lace. Doll wears cameo at collar opening. Hands are bisque, and jointed body is silk-twill covered. She poses with flowers and sheep before English countryside.

Resource List

MATERIALS AND SUPPLIES

Create-a-Doll
146 E. Chubbuck Rd.
Chubbuck, ID 83202
(208) 238-0433
Cork for stuffing.

Creative Silk
820 Oakdale Rd.
Atlanta, GA 30307
Dress fabrics.

Doll and Craft World, Inc.
125 Eighth St.
Brooklyn, NY 11215
Mohair wigs, books and patterns.

Dolls by Dottie
2910 Centerville
Dallas, TX 75228
Wigs and shoes.

Dollspart Supply Co., Inc.
5-15 49th Ave.
Long Island City, NY 11101
Doll stands, wigs, eyes, shoes and other supplies.

Fabrics for Historical Buildings
By Jane Nylander, 1983
Published by National Trust for Historic Preservation
Information on where to find documented fabrics.

Frank's Silhouette Parisian
P.O. Box 5
Laverne, CA 91750
Dress patterns.

Handcrafted by Dunstan
P.O. Box 9685
Denver, CO 80209
(303) 777-2054
Fine brown or white cabretta-leather bodies.

Hobby House Press
900 Frederich St.
Cumberland, MD 21502
(301) 759-3770
Patterns and books.

International Old Laces, Inc.
Martha Frey—Membership Chairman
4212 Bel Pre Rd.
Rockville, MD 20883
Lace making.

Laces
2982 Adeline St.
Berkeley, CA 94705
(415) 845-7178
Laces, lace-making equipment, tatting equipment, antique linen, silk pongee, silk crepe, Swiss batiste, silk crepelene, thread and needles.

Lyn's Doll House
Box 8341 DA
Denver, CO 80201
Patterns.

Marty's House of Dolls
Rt. 4, Box 108
Carmi, IL 62821
(618) 382-2209
Doll repairs.

Mays Ceramics
15041 Leffingwell
Whittier, CA 90604
(213) 941-5375
Paperweight eyes.

Schoepher
138 W. 31st St.
New York, NY 10001
Old eyes.

Terry's Leather Goods, Inc.
4965 S. Broadway
Denver, CO 80110
(303) 781-0121
Leather.

White, Lucy
P.O. Box 982
Westbrook, CT 06498
Mohair and lambskin for wigs.

DEALER LIST

Below is a list of dealers, with addresses and telephone numbers, from whom we have purchased French fashion dolls. Each has been considerate and reliable. (We have not intentionally left anyone off the list.) Most dealers do business by telephone and will ship dolls with a 3-day-return-privilege. Dealers also attend various doll shows; some dealers listed do business *only* at doll shows. Some dealers have doll lists, and some have display ads in doll magazines.

Cohen, Marcia
Cohen Auctions
P.O. Box 425—Rtes. 20-22
New Lebanon, NY 12125
(518) 794-7477
Most Cohen auctions contain some fine French fashion dolls.

Confederate Dollers
P.O. Box 24485
New Orleans, LA 70124
(504) 488-2967
Sells dolls at doll shows.

Fernando, Jim
370 Fair Oaks St.
San Francisco, CA 94110
(415) 282-9967
Sells dolls at doll shows. Also dresses dolls.

Harten, Helen
Red Door Antiques
Prescott, AZ 86031
(602) 445-4691
Carries selection of French fashion dolls.

Haynes, Mickie
4238 N. 7th Ave.
Phoenix, AZ 85013
(602) 264-1186
Has doll furniture for props and dolls.

Kaner, Jackie
9420 Reseda Blvd.
Northridge, CA 91325
Sells dolls at doll shows.

Kimport Dolls
P.O. Box 495
Independence, MO 64051
(816) 833-0517
Sells dolls by mail order or at doll shows. Publishes Doll Talk.

Left: Large doll, marked *F.G.,* appears to be in fashionable, all-original, perhaps mother-made, costume. Dress is fitted in bodice, and skirt is full. Costume is made of ruby satin. Long-sleeved jacket is embroidered and edged in gathered, pointed black lace. Underclothing is original.

Luzzi, Marlene
4 Fernwood Way
San Rafael, CA 94901
(415) 454-7164
Sells dolls by mail order or at doll shows.

Martin, Marshall and Don Christenson
45 Eucalyptus Knoll
Mill Valley, CA 94941
Sells dolls by mail order or at doll shows. Dresses some dolls.

McIntyre, Elizabeth
P.O. Box 105, RT 183
Colebrook, CT 06021
(203) 379-4726
Sells dolls at doll shop or doll shows.

Melton, Julia
P.O. Box 13311
Chesapeake, VA 23325
(804) 420-5117 or 420-9226
Sells dolls by mail order.

Ralph's Antique Dolls
7 Main St.
Parksville, MO 64152
(816) 741-3120 or 741-7699
Sells dolls at doll shows. Has doll shop and museum.

Richard Right Antiques
P.O. Box 187
Birchrunville, PA 19411
(215) 827-7442
Sells dolls by mail order, at doll shows and doll shop.

Robbins, Carolyn
Sells dolls at doll shows.

Rockwell, Karen
Sells dolls at doll shows.

Tarnowska, Maree
Narlingham
Surrey, England
Sells dolls at doll shows; brings unusual things from London.

Tyrrell, Billie Nelson
P.O. Box 1000
Studio City, CA 91604
Sells dolls at doll shows.

West, Ruth
1 N. Main St.
Parksville, MO 64152
(816) 741-5701
Sells dolls at doll shop and doll shows.

DOLL MUSEUMS

Below is a list of doll museums you may want to visit. Some of these museums have French fashion dolls, and others do not. Some museums are only open part of the year. So before you visit, be sure to contact them to see what they display in the museum and when they're open.

Adirondack Center Museum
Court St.
Elizabethtown, NY 12932

Alfred P. Sloan Museum
1221 E. Kearsley St.
Flint, MI 48503

Angels Attic
516 Colorado Ave.
Santa Monica, CA 90401

Anita's Doll Museum & Boutique
6737 Vesper Ave.
Van Nuys, CA 91405

Antique Doll Museum
1721 Broadway
Galveston, TX

Aunt Lens Doll & Toy Museum
6 Hamilton Terrace
New York, NY 10031

Bazaar Cada Dia
2801 Leavenworth
San Francisco, CA 94133

Brooklyn Children's Museum
145 Brooklyn Ave.
Brooklyn, NY 11213

Cameron's Doll & Carriage Museum
218 Becker's Lane
Manitou Springs, CO 80829

Camp McKensie Doll Museum
Mudo, SD 57559

Children's Museum
3000 N. Meridian St.
Indianapolis, IN 46206

Children's Museum
300 Congress St.
Boston, MA 02210

Children's Museum
67 E. Kirbey
Detroit, MI 48202

Christine's Doll Museum
4940 E. Speedway
Tucson, AZ 85712

Cotonlandia Museum
P.O. Box 1635
Greenwood, MS 38930

Crafty Owl Shop & Doll Museum
470 Washington Ave. N.
New Haven, CT 06512

Cupids Bow Doll Museum
958 Cambridge Ave.
Sunnyvale, CA 94087

Diminutive Doll Domain
Box 757
Indian Brook Rd.
Greene, NY 13778

Disney Dolls Museum
Grand Lake'O the Cherokees
Disney, OK 74340

Doll Cabinet & Museum
Star Rt., Box 221
Ferriday, LA 71334

Doll Castle Doll Museum
37 Belvedere Ave.
Washington, NJ 07882

Doll Museum & Trading Post
Highway 30
Legrand, IA 50142

Doll Museum at Anne Le Ceglis
5000 Calley
Norfolk, VA 23508

Dolls Den & Museum
406 River Ave.
Point Pleasant Beach, NJ 08742

Dolls in Wonderland
9 King St.
St. Augustine, FL 32084

Dolly Wares Doll Museum
3620 101 North
Florence, OR 97439

1840 Doll House Museum
196 Whitfield
Guilford, CT 06437

Enchanted World Doll Museum
Sioux Falls, South Dakota

Essie's Doll Museum
Rt. 16, Beech Bend Rd.
Bowling Green, KY 42101

Fairbanks Doll Museum
Hall Rd. (off Rt. 131)
Sturbridge, MA

Fairhaven Doll Museum
384 Alden Rd.
Fairhaven, MA 02719

Gay 90's Button & Doll Museum
Rt. 1, Box 78
Eureka Springs, AR 72632

Gerwecks Doll Museum
6299 Dixon Rd.
Monroe, MI 48161

Geuther's Doll Museum
188 N. Main St.
Eureka Springs, AR 72632

Ginny's Doll Shop and Museum
1117 S. Florida Ave.
Lakeland, FL 33803

Good Fairy Doll Museum
205 Walnut Ave.
Cranford, NJ 07016

Right: Fine 22-1/2-inch Portrait Jumeau wears couturier-made costume of gold-and-blue iridescent silk-taffeta. Interesting handmade, self-fabric edging decorates dress. Double rows of lace fall from inside sleeve and are gathered at neck. Hands are bisque, and body is leather.

Greenfield Village & Museum
Oakwood Blvd.
Dearborn, MI 48121

Hawley Rose Museum
305 E. Filer St.
Ludington, MI 49431

Heirloom Doll Hospital/Shop/Museum
416 E. Broadway
Waukesha, WI 53186

Helen Moe Antique Doll Museum
Hwy. 101 and Wellsona Rd.
Paso Robles, CA 93446

Hennepin County Historical Society
2303 Third Ave. South
Minneapolis, MN 55404

Hidden Magie Museum
4015 California
Norco, CA 91760

Hobby Horse Doll/Toy Museum
5310 Junius
Dallas, TX 78214

Homosassa Doll Museum
Rt. 5, Box 145
Homosassa, FL 32646

Jacksonville Doll Museum
5th & California St.
Jacksonville, OR 97530

Jonaires Doll & Toy Museum
Rt. 4, Box 4476
Stroudsburg, PA 18360

Kentucky Museum
Western Kentucky University
Bowling Green, KY 42101

Klehms Pink Peony Doll
2 E. Algonquin Rd.
Arlington Heights, IL 60005

Knotts Berry Farm Miniature Museum
8039 Beach Blvd.
Buena Park, CA 90261

Lolly's Doll & Toy Museum
225 Magazine St.
Galena, IL 61036

Madame Alexander's Doll Museum
711 S. 3rd Ave.
Chatsworth, GA 30705

Magic Mountain Doll Museum
Big Bear Lake, CA 92315

Margaret Woodbury Strong
1 Manhattan Square
Rochester, NY 14607

McCurdy Historical Doll Museum
246 N. 100 East
Provo, UT 84601

Memory Lane Doll & Toy Museum
Old Mystic Village
Mystic, CT 06355

Mary Merritt Doll Museum
Rt. 2
Douglassville, PA 19518

Milan Historica Museum
10 Edison Dr.
Milan, OH 44846

Museum of Antique Dolls
505 E. President St.
Savannah, GA 31401

Museum of Collectable Dolls
1117 S. Florida Ave.
Lakeland, FL 33803

Museum of Science & Industry
57th Street
Chicaco, IL 60637

Neill Museum
P.O. Box 801
Fort Davis, TX 79734

Old Brown House Doll Museum
1421 Ave. F
Gothenburg, NE 69138

Old Rectory
50 W. New England
Worthington, OH 43085

Playhouse Museum Old Dolls & Toys
1201 N. 2nd St.
Las Cruces, NM 88005

Pioneer Museum
215 S. Tejon
Colorado Springs, CO 80903

Poor Doll's Shop Museum
RR 2, Box 58
Syracuse, IN 46567

Portland Museum of Art
7 Congress Square
Portland, ME 04101

Santa Barbara Museum of Art
1130 State St.
Santa Barbara, CA 93101

Society of Memories Doll Museum
813 N. 2nd St.
St. Joseph, MO 64502

Space Farms Zoo & Museum
RFD 6, Box 135
Sussex, NJ 07460

Storybook Museum
620 Louis St.
Kerrville, TX 78028

Thomas County Museum
1525 W. 4th St.
Colby, KS 67701

Time Was Village Museum
Rt. 51 (4 miles south)
Mendota, IL 61342

Town of Yorktown Museum & Shop
1974 Commerce St.
Yorktown Heights, NY 10598

Toy Museum of Atlanta
2800 Peachtree Rd. N.E.
Atlanta, GA 30305

Treasure House Doll Museum
1215 W. Will Rogers
Claremore, OK 74017

University Historical Museum
Illinois State University
Normal, IL 61761

Victorian Doll Museum
4332 Buffalo Rd., Rt. 33
Rochester, NY 14514

Washington Dolls' House Museum
5236 44th St. NW
Washington, DC 20015

Wenham Historical Museum
132 Main St.
Wenham, MA 01984

White House Doll & Toy Museum
1238 S. Beach Blvd.
Anaheim, CA 92804

Wilkinsons Museum
3076 Morningside Dr.
Salt Lake City, UT 84124

Yesteryears Doll Museum
Main & River Sts.
Sandwich, MA 02563

Conversion to Metric Measure

When You Know	Symbol	Multiply By	To Find	Symbol
VOLUME				
teaspoons	tsp.	4.93	milliliters	ml
tablespoons	tbsp.	14.79	milliliters	ml
fluid ounces	fl. oz.	29.57	milliliters	ml
cups	c.	0.24	liters	l
pints	pt.	0.47	liters	l
quarts	qt.	0.95	liters	l
gallons	gal.	3.79	liters	l
LENGTH				
inches	in.	2.54	centimeters	cm
feet	ft.	30.48	centimeters	cm
yards	yd.	0.91	meters	m
TEMPERATURE				
Fahrenheit	F	0.56 (after subtracting 32)	Celsius	C

Left: 17-inch wood-bodied Rohmer doll has bisque hands and feet. She wears full-skirted dress of beige satin-striped silk. Material is machine-embroidered with gold-cord roses. Sleeves are puffed at shoulders and tighter in lower arm. She wears early flat-heeled leather slippers with gold buckle on front.

Index

Left: Parisienne dressed in original winter outfit. Doll came in antique box, complete with moths. She is 18 inches tall. Her leather-covered, jointed wood body has bisque hands. Lower legs are kid, stuffed with sawdust. Toes are sewn in. Unmarked doll has "collar" shoulderplate. Ears are unpierced. Pate is cork, and blond wig is coarse human hair. Plum-colored, three-piece wool dress is completely lined with glazed brown fabric. Full skirt is made with modified train. Overskirt is draped in back and trimmed with fringe and two narrow widths of black and brown velvet ribbon. Black-velvet hat is decorated with plum ribbon and brown plush. Doll wears artificial-fur neckpiece and muff. She wears hand-stitched split drawers, chemise and back-laced corset with stays. Petticoat is fully gathered. Stockings are hand-knit, and brown leather boots have high heels.